GunDigest Illustrated Guide to

MODERN FIREARMS

Edited by Jennifer L.S. Pearsall

Published by

Gun Digest® Books, an imprint of F+W Media, Inc.
Krause Publications • 700 East State Street • Iola, WI 54990-0001
715-445-2214 • 888-457-2873
www.krausebooks.com

To order books or other products call toll-free 1-800-258-0929
or visit us online at www.gundigeststore.com

ISBN-13: 978-1-4402-3253-4
ISBN-10: 1-4402-3253-9

Designed by Dusty Reid
Edited by Jennifer L.S. Pearsall

Printed in United States of America

WELCOME TO THE *GUN DIGEST ILLUSTRATED GUIDE TO MODERN FIREARMS!*

Because looking at fabulous pictures of all the world's guns is part of what the staff here at *Gun Digest* books gets to do every day as part of our jobs, you might think we'd get tired of it. Well, you might think that, but you'd be wrong. In fact, if we didn't have to get around to putting pictures of all the neato-keen guns we stumble across into a book like this one, we'd probably never stop surfing the web and gazing at every new ounce of firepower to hit the market. But stop we did, and make a book we did, one we hope gives our readers a magnum dose of the firearm eye-candy we are fortunate enough to work with every day.

Whether you're a hobbiest, a serious competitor, a custom gun collector, or one of the newest members to the shooting sports and our family, we know that if you have half as much fun turning the pages of *Illustrated Guide to Modern Firearms* as we did putting them together, then you're going to have a ball with this book. Remember, at *Gun Digest*, we know guns so you know guns, and we hope these pages inspire everyone out there to try a new gun, try a new shooting sport, teach a new shooter what it's all about, and get involved.

Happy reading and straight shooting!

—*Jennifer L.S. Pearsall, Editor*

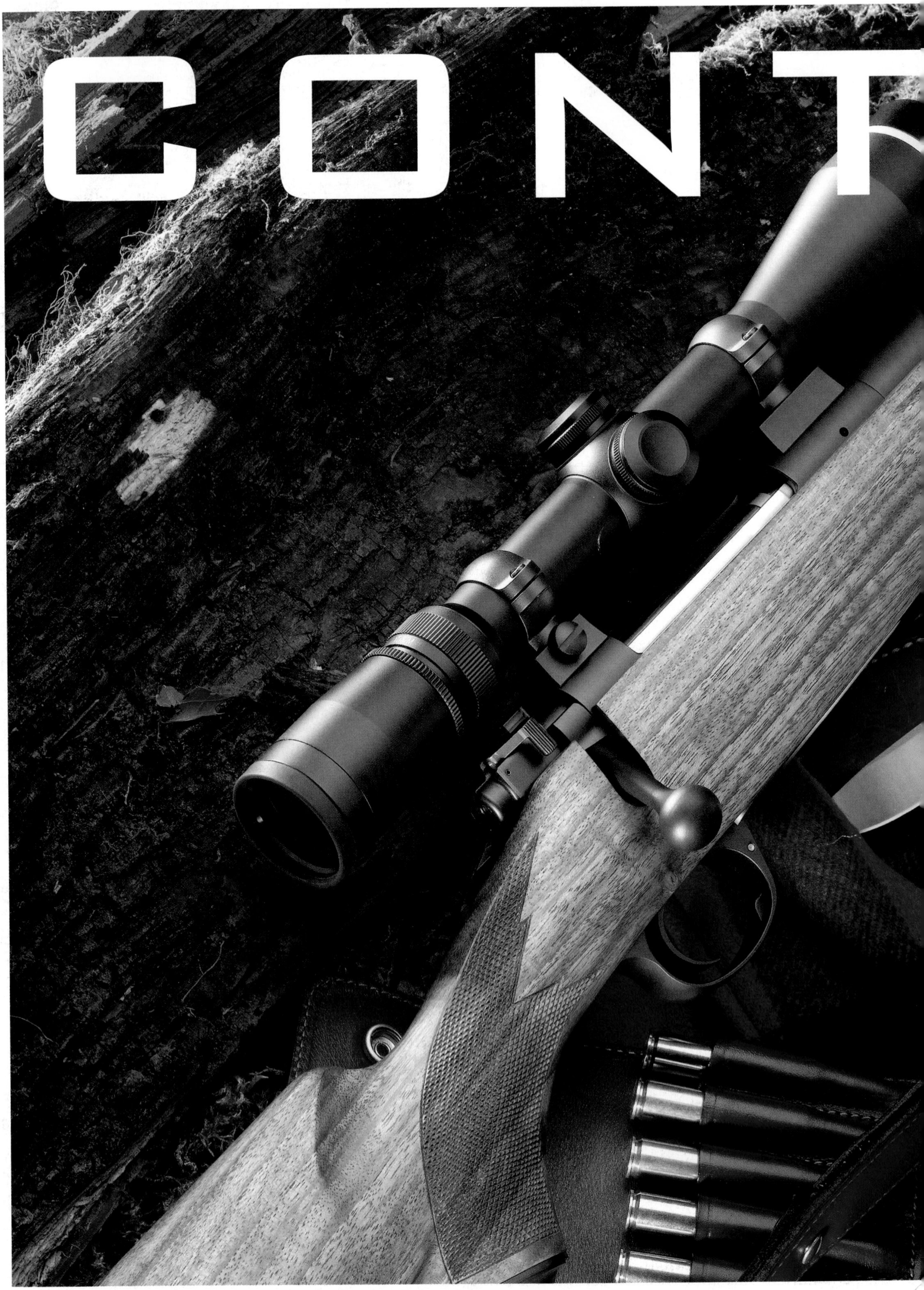
CONT

ENTS

CHAPTER 1

SPECIALTY TACTICAL

Not every tactical rifle is built on the AR platform. Special circumstances call for special weapons with special capabilities. The operators who use these rifles go by several names: "Designated Marksman," "Sharpshooter," "Scout," and the ever-popular "Sniper." The one common element linking all these titles together is the use of a specialized rifle to complete a specific task.

More often than not, the assumption is that special-purpose rifles are used for long-range shooting to neutralize distant targets with surgical accuracy. This may be true in some cases and, as such, the rifle used for these operations certainly needs to be a precision implement. But the truth of the matter is, the average law-enforcement "sniper" shot is taken from a distance of less than 100 yards. And, in a special operations role, the rifle may be called on to engage a barricaded subject, quietly neutralize enemy personnel or equipment, or operate in physical environments that would render other weapons useless. These rifles are created for specific circumstances and employed by specialized personnel to best obtain a very specifically desired result.

While each of these weapons platforms will sport varying options to meet specific needs, some of the common elements found on all of them will include tighter tolerances, carefully crafted bolt lock-up to ensure full contact, match-grade barrels (nearly always free-floated), adjustable stocks that provide perfect and easily repeatable fit, adjustable triggers, and accessory rails that allow many sighting system options. Many of these rifles will also come equipped with or ready to accept a suppressor.

The goal with these exacting firearms is to ensure that each individual operator can create a weapons platform that offers the greatest chance of success in a very demanding environment. In many cases, and especially at long range, even the slightest imperfection can mean the difference between a hit and a miss. To obtain the highest performance levels, gun makers use the utmost care in crafting their products, including hand fitting and an individual attention to detail that turn the finest raw materials into a precision-crafted rifle. This combination is often reflected in the prices of these rifles. While there are some exceptions to the rule and you will find a few top performers in, shall we call it, the "affordable" category, most of the time you will get what you pay for.

If you carry a gun for a living, you might want to look into one of these fine rifles as one of the tools of your trade. Any rifle on this list will get the job done, though some are designed for extremely special jobs. It is up to you to choose the right tool. If you simply love outstanding performance from a top-notch piece of hardware, you could pretty much start anywhere on the pages that follow and enhance your firepower with one of these beauties (though it's worth noting that, with a few of these special-purpose rifles, plinking could turn out to be quite expensive).

While some of the rifles presented here fall under NFA rules, many more are available in civilian-legal versions that can be purchased from appropriate dealers without any additional federal paperwork. And, if you absolutely must have a suppressor or a short barrel, the paperwork to get one is really not all that onerous.

Flip through these pages with the expectation of finding something special. You won't be disappointed. But remember, this is simply an overview. There is no way we could capture all the data on all the rifles available for and in this segment. If your mission requires a special-purpose rifle, chances are very good you can find something somewhere that will fit.

—*Kevin Michalowski, Editor,* Gun Digest *magazine*

KIMBER MODEL 8400 ADVANCED TACTICAL

The Kimber Model 8400 Advanced Tactical Rifle is built by hand in limited quantities. Each has a match-grade barrel, chamber, and trigger, along with a trued bolt face, hand-finished chamber, lapped lugs, and custom glass bedding. Additional special features include an extended bolt handle with enlarged knob, and a Picatinny rail with integral 20 MOA elevation.

Recently, an all-black model in .308 Winchester was added to the line. The original version has a desert camouflage pattern stock and dark earth metal finish. It is available in both .308 Winchester and .300 Winchester Magnum. All Advanced Tactical rifles have the premium KimPro II metal finish, which is non-reflective, self-lubricating, and extremely resistant to moisture and salt. The guns wear McMillan A-5 fully adjustable stocks that have a positive stippled texture, a bipod stud, and four flush QD sling swivel cups. Other standard features include a three-position Model 70-type wing safety, floorplate with release button inside the trigger guard, and a full-length Mauser claw extractor for true controlled-round feeding and extraction. Each rifle is shipped in a Pelican hard case.

ABOVE

MCMILLAN TAC-50 A1-R2

The recoil on a .50 BMG rifle can be stout. McMillan has cut that by 90 percent with a new hydraulic recoil mitigation system in its TAC-50. At the heart of the TAC-50 A1-R2 recoil mitigation system is a proprietary hydraulic piston in the buttstock. As the rifle is fired, the piston compresses, softening the recoil by lowering the peak recoil force and spreading out the entire recoil sensation over several milliseconds. Without the R2 recoil mitigation system, the peak recoil from a .50 BMG cartridge is approximately 7,500 pounds of force. From start to finish, the recoil lasts one millisecond in a machine rest. With the R2 system, though, the peak recoil is only about 520 pounds of force. What's more, the force is spread out over six milliseconds—which may look tiny, but is, in reality, much longer than the original recoil force. The proprietary muzzle brake offered on the TAC-50 A1-R2 also provides additional recoil reduction.

The TAC-50 A1-R2 also features a new take-down A1-style fiberglass stock with a fore-end that is five inches longer than the original TAC-50 stock, moving the balance point for the bipod forward. There is a saddle-type cheekpiece, and the removable buttstock is attached to the rifle with a quick-detach pushpin. The stock incorporates a smaller pistol grip designed to accommodate a wider range of hand shapes, both with and without gloves.

The TAC-50 A1-R2 has a new bipod that is lighter and sturdier than the original TAC-50's. The legs adjust vertically, as well as back and forth. A new magazine system offers a positive, self-locking latch that's easier to operate with gloves. The magazine release lever is repositioned ahead of the trigger bow.

As with the original TAC-50, the TAC-50 A1-R2 features a 29-inch premium, hand-lapped, match-grade, free-floating barrel, threaded muzzle brake, detachable five-round box magazine, tuned 3½-pound trigger, and extra-long bolt handle for large optics clearance. All components are built to benchrest precision tolerances.

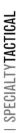

BELOW

MCMILLAN TAC-308

The TAC-308 is designed for urban tactical scenarios. It is chambered in .308 Winchester and 6.5 Creedmoor and wears a heavy, match-grade stainless steel barrel. The McMillan tactical rifle stock features a spacer system, flush-mount swivel cups, and integral adjustable cheekpiece. The TAC-308A variant includes an A3-5 stock with detachable box magazine and a 20-inch barrel, while the TAC-308B version includes an A3-5 stock with detachable box magazine and 24-inch barrel. To produce the phenomenal accuracy these rifles are known for, barrel threads and chamber are cut to critical tolerances and fit by hand. The barrel axis is perfectly in line with the bolt axis, and the bolt and action faces are perpendicular to the barrel axis. The action is pillar-bedded into the stock, and the barrel is free-floated. All dimensions are held to competition benchrest standards. Second only to the hand fitting of a great barrel to a great action, the trigger is paramount to top-notch accuracy. To that end, the TAC-308 offers a tuned three-pound trigger that can be adjusted by any-competent gunsmith.

VENOM TACTICAL TAIPAN

The Venom Tactical Taipan is designed for extreme long-range operations, with its .338 Lapua round delivering deadly performance out past 1,800 yards. It utilizes a Remington long-action receiver blueprinted to Venom Tactical's exacting tolerances; lock-up is tight and secure. Like all Venom Tactical rifles, the Taipan's bolt is of Venom's elliptical design and machined and ground from 4340.

The Taipan is equipped with a Brux barrel made to Venom Tactical specifications. The barreled action is firmly mounted to a Manners composite T-4A stock with a textured fore-end and palm swell. The stock also allows for an adjustable cheek weld and is designed for shooting from the prone position. It includes a one-inch Decelerator butt pad and a five-round detachable box magazine, and the package is shipped with a Venom Antidote muzzle brake installed. This rifle gives you everything you need in a long-range sniper platform and nothing you don't.

SIG SAUER SSG 3000

The SIG SSG 3000 has a modular design that not only provides ease of maintenance, but also the ability for the end user to easily replace the barrel, thereby eliminating costly gunsmithing expenses. These barrels are heavy-contoured, hammer forged, and fitted with a flash suppressor/muzzle brake to provide greater accuracy and reduced muzzle signature.

A massive six-lug lockup system is used to give the SSG 3000 greater strength and accuracy, while the light-weight firing pin means an extremely short lock time, something in the range of three milliseconds. The steel receiver and bolt are both precision-machined to exact tolerances, and the bolt locks directly into the chamber, eliminating headspace concerns.

The ergonomic qualities of the SSG 3000 are exceptional. The tough McMillan composite stock is designed with a comfortable pistol grip and fully adjustable stock to give the shooter a custom fit and to encourage a natural shooting position that facilitates comfort and concentration over long periods of time without fatigue or distraction. The trigger is adjustable for position, take up, let-off point, and pull weight. Chambered in .308 Win., this rifle will fill the role of the urban police or military sniper nicely, with an effective range of more than 800 meters.

SIG SAUER TACTICAL 2

The Tactical 2 is the most advanced version of the precision rifle ever developed by Blaser/SIG Sauer. Each design element was driven by the requirement to create the best shooting platform possible. Exceptional accuracy was one of the key goals during development, with effective engagement ranges of 1,500 meters or more, depending on caliber and ammunition. Advanced engineering and uncompromising quality are evident in every facet of this rifle's design.

The Tactical 2 is a bolt-action rifle featuring Blaser's revolutionary straight-pull action. When the bolt is closed, the 360-degree radial collet expands into the locking groove in the barrel; the bolt head is auto-centering and self-headspacing. The straight-pull action is, naturally, absent rotating parts, which assures rapid extraction and reloading with minimal movement. The rifle can easily be converted for left- or right-hand shooters, and it also allows for the exchange of calibers by replacing the barrel and bolt head, in under a minute, without special tools and with no change in accuracy.

Barrels are cold hammer-forged, fluted, and plasma-nitride treated to provide maximum resistance against corrosion and abrasion. An M1913 Picatinny rail is fixed to the barrel, for full compatibility with a wide range of optical sighting systems. The muzzle end is threaded for an optional brake. The receiver is machined from aircraft-grade billet aluminum alloy and is the interface for the barrel, bolt assembly, trigger assembly, and magazine. A recoil lug of hardened steel is integrated into the receiver. The entire unit is fixed to the stock, eliminating temperature-induced distortion. The outer surface is hard anodized, and the ergonomically correct stock is injection molded out of fiber-reinforced polymers and is absolutely stable, even under extreme temperatures. The Tactical 2 is offered in .223 Remington, .308 WIN, .300 Win. Mag. and .338 Lapua.

LEFT

BARRETT MRAD

Can one rifle do it all? The Barrett MRAD just might. This bolt-action is defining a whole new class of long-range rifles.

The heart of the MRAD is the rifle's user-changeable barrel system. The precision-grade barrel can be removed by simply unscrewing two bolts via a standard Torx wrench. Besides reducing maintenance and logistical burdens, this unique design paves the way for future caliber interchangeability and serviceability. The base rifle is offered in .338 Lapua, and barrels for .300 Winchester Magnum and .308 Winchester are in the pipeline.

The MRAD also boasts Barrett's new easily accessed trigger module. This match-grade trigger is drop fire-proof and combat ready. The thumb-operated safety can be configured for left- or right-handed operation, and the ambidextrous magazine release can be used intuitively while retaining the grip and cheek weld.

Integrated into the MRAD rifle's 7000 series aluminum upper receiver is an M1913 rail with 30 MOA taper and 21.75 inches of rail space. The MRAD rifle's stock is foldable for enhanced portability, yet locks in as solid as a fixed-stock rifle to create a rigid platform for consistent firing. When folded, the stock latches around the bolt handle for added security during transport. The rifle's length of pull can be set to five different positions with the push of a single button.

BELOW

BARRETT M107A1

The newest .50 BMG sniper rifle from Barrett may be related to the Model 82A1/M107, but the M107A1 is far from a simple evolution of its ancestors. Driven by the demands of combat, every component was re-engineered to be lighter yet stronger. The result is a high-performance rifle that weighs four pounds less than the original M107, but is every bit as tough.

Designed to be used with a suppressor, the M107A1 allows operators to combine signature reduction capabilities with flawless reliability. An all-new bolt carrier group is key to making the rifle suppressor-ready, and its titanium four-port muzzle brake is engineered to work seamlessly with a quick-attach Barrett .50 BMG Suppressor.

Inside the lightweight aluminum upper receiver, the bolt carrier rides on a hardened steel, anti-wear strip for added durability. The bolt carrier's components are protected with a mix of ultra-hard PVD coatings and advanced nickel Teflon plating that increases lubricity, is corrosion-resistant, and greatly eases cleaning. The rear barrel stop and front barrel bushing are bolted and bonded with a compound similar to that used on space shuttles. A titanium barrel key and fully chrome-lined bore and chamber add to the rifle's durability. This is, without doubt, a rifle built for the extreme duty required in modern combat.

ABOVE

ACCURACY INTERNATIONAL AX338

Based on the DNA of the battle-proven AW series, the advanced, new-generation AX338 bolt-action inherits all the toughness, reliability, superb accuracy, and ease of maintenance of its celebrated predecessor. The AX rifle's magnum action retains the same flat-bottomed design, but is longer and wider to facilitate a compact and reliable double-stack 10-round magazine for the .338 Lapua rounds. Features include an improved external stock design, available with either a pistol or thumb-hole configuration, and a versatile fore-end rail system for fitting a variety of optical, ranging, support, and carrying accessories. This design improves the operator's ability to carry and move with the rifle, and the shorter rear stock allows for comfortable shooting while wearing bulky body armor.

The AX 338 is optimized for .338 Lapua rounds firing 300-grain projectiles. Permanently bonding and bolting the action to the assembly maintains zero in the harshest conditions. The new modular bolt is now .87-inches in diameter, making it, the bolt head, locking ring, and barrel tenon capable of withstanding higher pressures and temperatures. A new leaf spring-style extractor provides easy removal and replacement.

Like all Accuracy International products, the free-floated barrel is threaded deeply into the action with a large diameter thread for durability. Several barrel lengths are available, and buyers can choose among rifling twists and muzzle brakes or threading for a suppressor, making the AX338 as close to custom as a buyer can get in a production rifle.

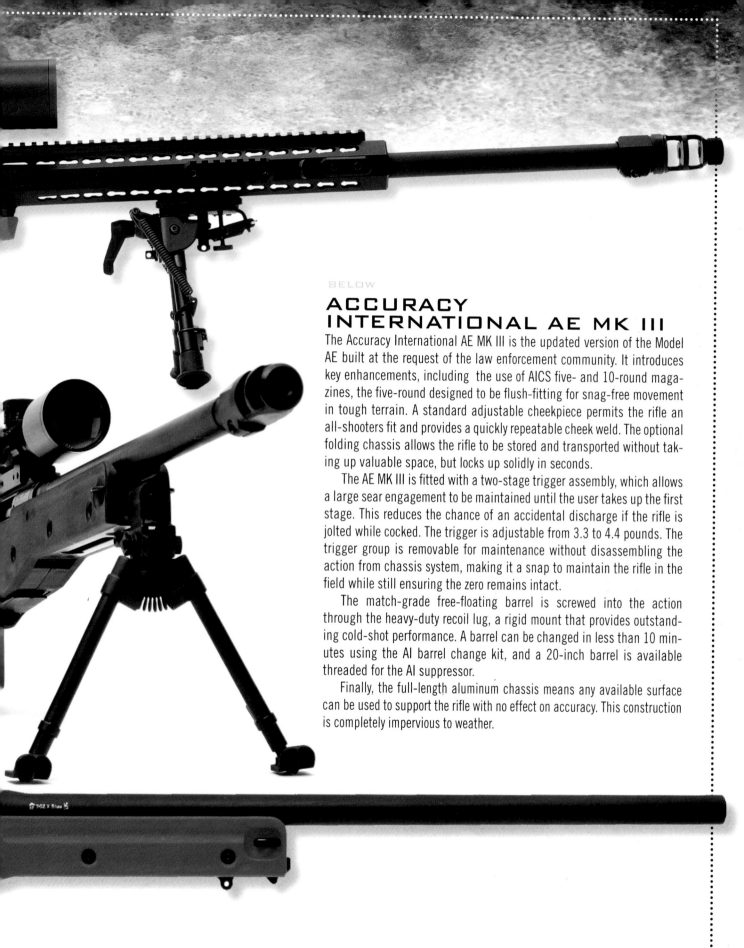

ACCURACY INTERNATIONAL AE MK III

The Accuracy International AE MK III is the updated version of the Model AE built at the request of the law enforcement community. It introduces key enhancements, including the use of AICS five- and 10-round magazines, the five-round designed to be flush-fitting for snag-free movement in tough terrain. A standard adjustable cheekpiece permits the rifle an all-shooters fit and provides a quickly repeatable cheek weld. The optional folding chassis allows the rifle to be stored and transported without taking up valuable space, but locks up solidly in seconds.

The AE MK III is fitted with a two-stage trigger assembly, which allows a large sear engagement to be maintained until the user takes up the first stage. This reduces the chance of an accidental discharge if the rifle is jolted while cocked. The trigger is adjustable from 3.3 to 4.4 pounds. The trigger group is removable for maintenance without disassembling the action from chassis system, making it a snap to maintain the rifle in the field while still ensuring the zero remains intact.

The match-grade free-floating barrel is screwed into the action through the heavy-duty recoil lug, a rigid mount that provides outstanding cold-shot performance. A barrel can be changed in less than 10 minutes using the AI barrel change kit, and a 20-inch barrel is available threaded for the AI suppressor.

Finally, the full-length aluminum chassis means any available surface can be used to support the rifle with no effect on accuracy. This construction is completely impervious to weather.

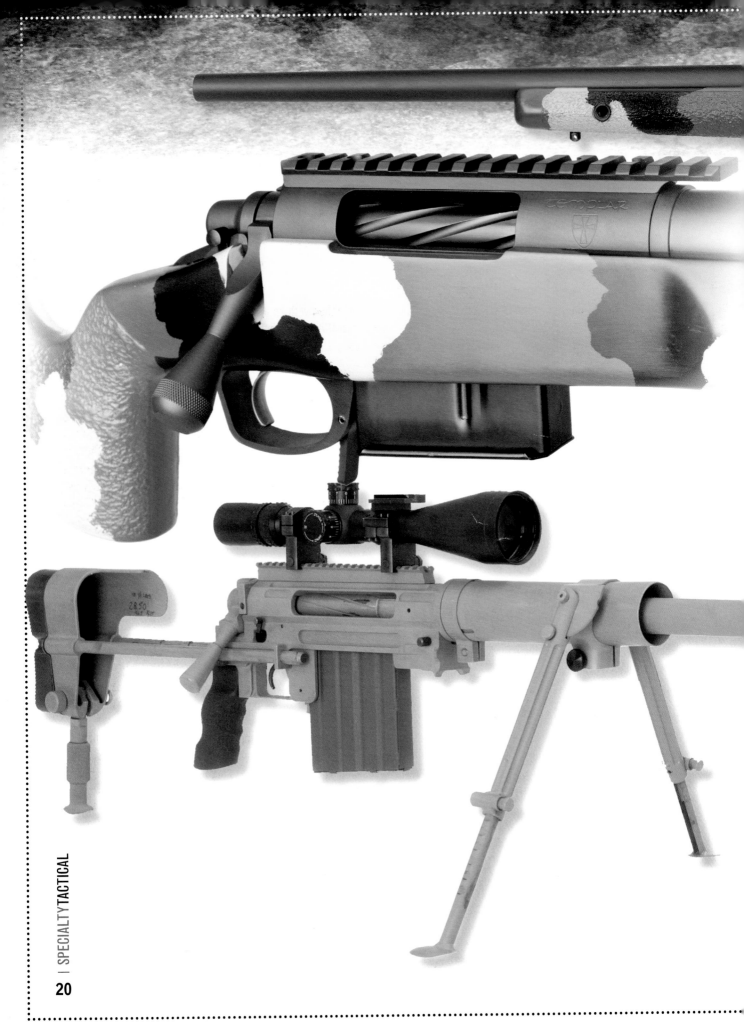

GA PRECISION CRUSADER

What's that cliché about building a better mousetrap? Well, GA Precision has applied that concept to the long-range tactical rifle, using what is basically the design of a Remington 700 action and taking it a couple steps beyond.

First up is the receiver body, which is hardened 416 stainless steel, while the tang is thicker and then radiused so it still fits a Model 700-style stock nicely. The precision-ground recoil lug is double-pinned. The steel 20 MOA base is attached with four 8-40 tapered-head grade 8 T-15 screws. The bolt stop has been changed to the GAP-style side release. The raceway is Wire ED-Med instead of broached.

Primary extraction is increased by 35 percent. This means that, upon opening the bolt, the case is pulled out of the chamber 35 per-cent more than with an unenhanced extraction. It makes for a very smooth bolt cycle. In the same vein, the bolt and bolt handle are now one piece, machined from a solid piece of 4320 CM and heat-treated. The knob is the only part that is threaded on via $^5/_{16}$x24 threads. The handle is swept back a tad for ease of operation. The extractors are M-16-type and stronger than other designs.

The standard caliber is .308 Winchester, but other calibers can be special ordered. The barrel is a 23-inch Bartlein stainless steel 5R rifling No. 7 GAP contour with a 1:11¼ twist. All this is nestled into a McMillan A5 stock covered in GAP camouflage with one stud and four flush cups. If you are moving up to the magnum calibers, the bolt is .750-inch in diameter for .338 Lapua and Rigby-based cartridges.

CHEYTAC M-200 INTERVENTION

The M-200 Intervention is as precise in manufacturing tolerances as any other specialty rifle. But, to ensure that they can get every bit of accuracy out of those outstanding platforms, CheyTac plunged into the world of mathematics to find the perfect balance for a bullet in flight.

CheyTac L.L.C researched the optimum cartridge and barrel configuration for very long-range accuracy. They worked with the now-defunct company Lost River Ballistic Technologies and developed the .408 CheyTac. Lost River Ballistic Technologies inventor Warren Jensen stated, "The .408 CheyTac is the first bullet/rifle system that utilizes a balanced flight projectile. To achieve balanced flight, the linear drag has to be balanced with the rotational drag to keep the very fine nose (meplat) of the bullet pointed directly into the oncoming air. It should result in very little precession and yaw at extreme range … ."

The process is a patented one in which a projectile engraved and launched according to the specifications should decelerate from supersonic flight through transonic to subsonic in a stable and predictable manner effective to a range beyond 3,000 yards (2,743 meters). To achieve this, the rifle barrel has to have rifling dimensions specific to achieving a desired amount of axial air drag on the bullet's surface, which reduces the bullet's spin rate to achieve balanced flight.

CheyTac asserts, "The CheyTac LRRS is a solid anti-personnel system to 2,000 yards (1,830 meters). The primary intent of the .408 is as an extreme-range anti-personnel system. Groups of seven to nine inches at 1,000 yards, 10 inches at 1500 yards and 15 inches at 2,000 yards have been consistently obtained." Now, put that in the 31-pound, 53-inch long M200 Intervention bolt-action, and we think the "enemy," whoever they may be in today's battlefields, would be smart to find a place to hide—very, very far away.

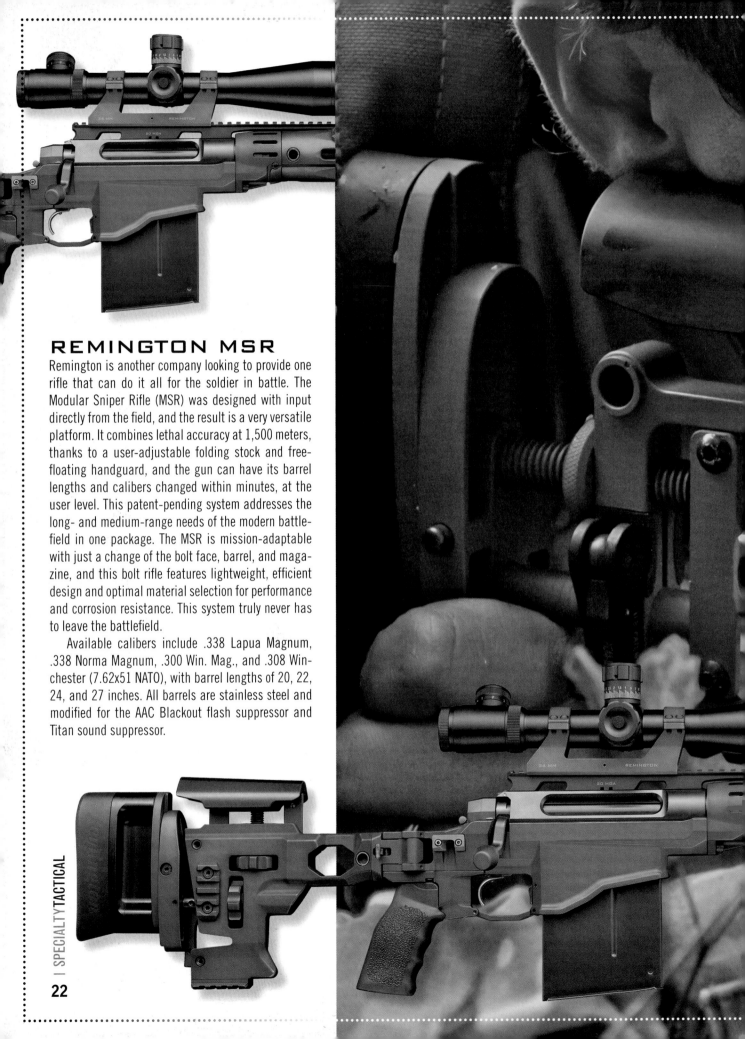

REMINGTON MSR

Remington is another company looking to provide one rifle that can do it all for the soldier in battle. The Modular Sniper Rifle (MSR) was designed with input directly from the field, and the result is a very versatile platform. It combines lethal accuracy at 1,500 meters, thanks to a user-adjustable folding stock and free-floating handguard, and the gun can have its barrel lengths and calibers changed within minutes, at the user level. This patent-pending system addresses the long- and medium-range needs of the modern battlefield in one package. The MSR is mission-adaptable with just a change of the bolt face, barrel, and magazine, and this bolt rifle features lightweight, efficient design and optimal material selection for performance and corrosion resistance. This system truly never has to leave the battlefield.

Available calibers include .338 Lapua Magnum, .338 Norma Magnum, .300 Win. Mag., and .308 Winchester (7.62x51 NATO), with barrel lengths of 20, 22, 24, and 27 inches. All barrels are stainless steel and modified for the AAC Blackout flash suppressor and Titan sound suppressor.

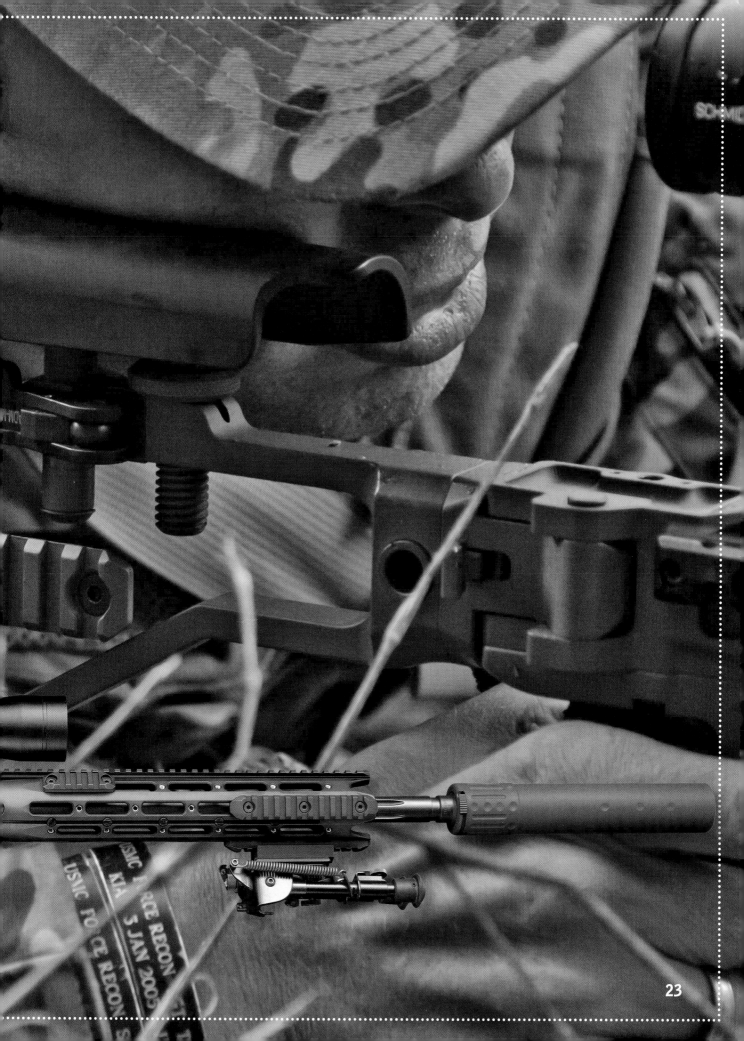

MCMILLAN CS5

The bolt-action McMillan CS5 is specifically designed as a compact and concealable precision tactical rifle for use primarily in urban settings. It is available in suppressed configuration for military and law enforcement applications, as well as standard configurations for the every day gun owner. The neatest thing about this one? The entire weapons system breaks down to fit inside a common backpack.

With the buttstock and suppressor detached, the CS5 is only 23 inches in overall length. It stuffs neatly into backpacks, duffel bags, and other inconspicuous carriers, yet it delivers the stopping authority of a .308 projectile and outstanding accuracy with either subsonic or full-power ammunition. Using McMillan's match-grade 200-grain subsonic .308 Winchester ammunition, the CS5 will deliver .75 MOA performance or better in close-quarters settings. With full-power match-grade ammunition, the CS5 will also deliver .75 MOA performance or better at typical 7.62 NATO distances, making it a truly dual-purpose firearm.

Designed with extensive input from elite military teams, the infinitely adjustable buttstock will fit any operator, regardless of height, build, bulk of clothing, or shooting position, and index marks allow easily repeatable stock adjustments. A tactile safety button can be operated without moving the trigger finger, and the Anschütz match trigger adjusts for weight and length of pull. Applicable NFA rules apply regarding SBR and suppressor.

25

FNH USA SCAR16

You either need to have a badge or be under the jurisdiction of the U.S. Military to get your hands on one of these, but the SCAR16 from FNH is fun to look at even if you don't qualify for possession of this Class III select-fire .223. (FYI—check out the 3-gun matches in your area and www.3gunnation.com, where FNH USA is a major player and often supplies SCAR16s and other guns it makes for competitors to shoot. Lots of fun even if you can't take them home at the end of the day!)

The gun has a cycle rate of 625 rounds per minute and a barrel life of 16,000 rounds. That may not actually be much in the heat of a long-waged war, but the barrel, which comes in three different lengths, can be switched out in under five minutes, and point of impact is guaranteed to shift less than a single MOA during swap-out. The adjustable cheekpiece stock telescopes and side folds for more compact transport in places like tanks, convoy trucks, and helicopters. The gun accepts standard M16 mags, and it's loaded with accessory rails at three, six, nine, and 12 o'clock. Just in case all that's not enough, the SCAR family includes the same three-barrel arrangement in .308, plus the MK13 variant EGLM, or Enhanced Grenade Launcher Module. Oh, and just in case you were wondering what SCAR stands for, it's short for Special Operations Forces Combat Assault Rifle. Yup, they left out "Operations Forces" to make the acronym, probably because SOFCAR doesn't sound nearly as ominous as SCAR. Fine marketing all around, don't you think?

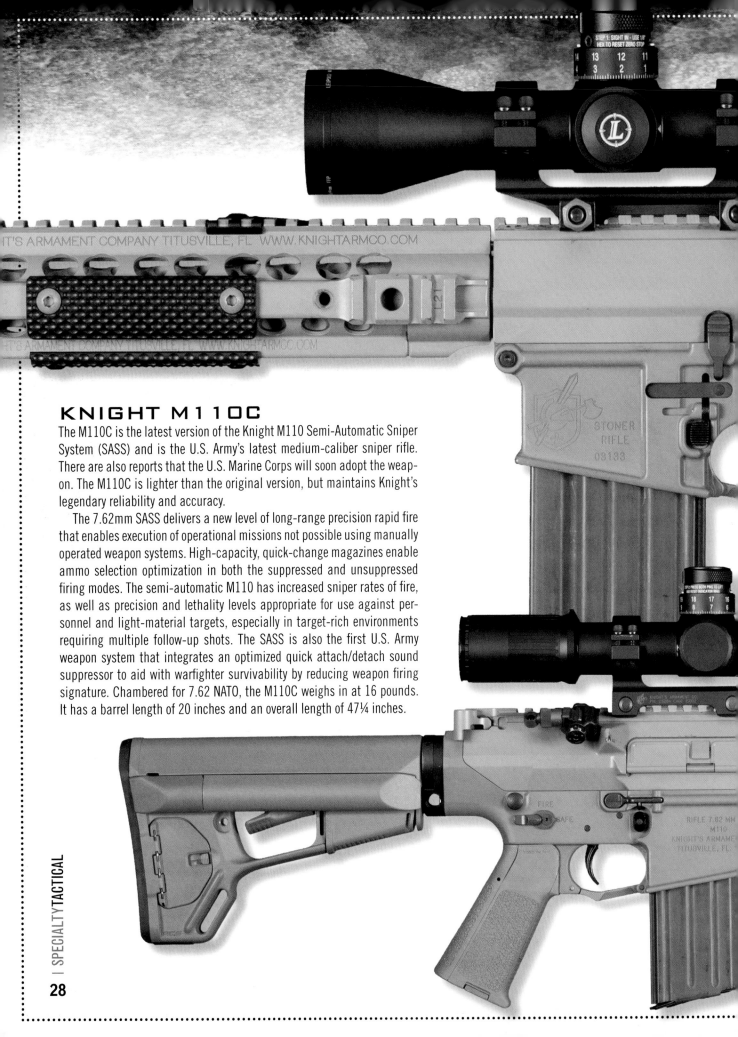

KNIGHT M110C

The M110C is the latest version of the Knight M110 Semi-Automatic Sniper System (SASS) and is the U.S. Army's latest medium-caliber sniper rifle. There are also reports that the U.S. Marine Corps will soon adopt the weapon. The M110C is lighter than the original version, but maintains Knight's legendary reliability and accuracy.

The 7.62mm SASS delivers a new level of long-range precision rapid fire that enables execution of operational missions not possible using manually operated weapon systems. High-capacity, quick-change magazines enable ammo selection optimization in both the suppressed and unsuppressed firing modes. The semi-automatic M110 has increased sniper rates of fire, as well as precision and lethality levels appropriate for use against personnel and light-material targets, especially in target-rich environments requiring multiple follow-up shots. The SASS is also the first U.S. Army weapon system that integrates an optimized quick attach/detach sound suppressor to aid with warfighter survivability by reducing weapon firing signature. Chambered for 7.62 NATO, the M110C weighs in at 16 pounds. It has a barrel length of 20 inches and an overall length of 47¼ inches.

CHAPTER 2

PISTOLS

With a plethora of semi-auto pistols flooding the market, one would think that gun companies couldn't possibly introduce any more new ones into this category. But, in reality, the opposite is actually the case. This is especially apparent in the ever-expanding and crowded field of the venerable 1911, which continues to vindicate the genius of John M. Browning's now century old design with newer and better incarnations. The 1911 is here to stay, and for good reason—it works. If imitation is the sincerest form of flattery, the 1911 remains the most flattered handgun design in history.

On the professional side, police agencies and militaries from around the globe are engaged in a never-ending search for pistols featuring operations-specific refinements. Driving competition in this field are features that afford the operator tactical advantages, no matter how slight, whether the theater be a war-torn battlefield or the mean streets of America.

Two such pistols are the Para 14-45 Black Ops and its little brother, the Para Stealth. It comes standard with aftermarket night sights and a new finish that's both tough and unassuming (in a covert sort of way). With slide rails facilitating the attachment of lights and lasers, these handguns cater to professionals operating in niche environments.

Semi-autos such as these exemplify the influence of real-world pros; they're plug-and-play for those who have mission-specific requirements, and yet these guns don't require any aftermarket machining or gunsmithing to be ready for prime time.

On the civilian side, political winds of change have brought increased opportunities for concealed carry. It seems everyone is shoving cold blue steel down their pants these days, and there's no shortage of companies eager to oblige. This positive trend is fueling the demand for small backup guns designed for deep conceal-ment. A fine example is the Colt New Agent, a pistol that comes in a variety of configurations, including a Crimson Trace laser grip version. This petite backup gun, chambered in the powerful .45 ACP, is a man-stopper. It does not have external sights, but, instead, a "trench-style" groove sight designed to make it easy to draw from hidden environs and still get on target when things get up close and personal. The Colt .380 Pocketlite, Taurus 22/25 PLY, and Kimber Solo CDP are among additional examples of tiny backup guns for self-defense recently introduced.

And then there are guns popular with both pros and civilians. Enter Glock, the polymer juggernaut that continues to whet its insatiable appetite for global domination. Now in its fourth generation (Gen4), the Austrian gun maker is expanding its empire by offering the simple perfection of the Glock in new calibers. For those with discriminating ballistic tastes or shooters who simply want to try something new, consider the new Glock 32 Gen4 in .357 SIG. Some have hailed this hot little number as ballistically superior to the popular .40 S&W, the chambering in Glock's G22, G23, and G27 guns. Still, others note the .357 SIG's higher cost-per-round and lesser availability. Time will tell how popular this cartridge (and others, like the .45 G.A.P.) become.

Finally, there are the semi-auto handguns that blend function and art. One can't help but stare dreamily at the gorgeous Kimber Classic Pro Carry, an Officer's-size 1911 with distinctive white bone grips that stand out against a Turnbull Restoration blued finish. This handgun has been described as a "gentleman's gun" and—with a price tag pushing $2,000—would be a fine match for a suit coat, high-end watch, and the best bottle of cabernet sauvignon money can buy. It's perfectly suited as one for a night out on the town, and is one of many new handguns for the handgun connoisseur who wants function but can't live without the beauty.

Corey Graff, Gun Digest Online Content 511

CABOT GUNS 1911

Cabot Guns is a new, American-made 1911 pistol company with roots in the aerospace machining industry. By using proprietary machine tools, the company boasts a frame-to-slide fit of .001-inch (.0005 per side), making them interchangeable between any other comparable 1911 pistol in the company's line up.

COLT NEW AGENT

The Colt New Agent is a compact big-bore semi-auto designed for deep—and we do mean deep—concealment. Despite being chambered in a sledgehammer of a cartridge (.45 ACP), it has a teensy little three-inch bushing-less barrel. You can yank it from your pants quick-like due to its smooth top slide and trench-style sights.

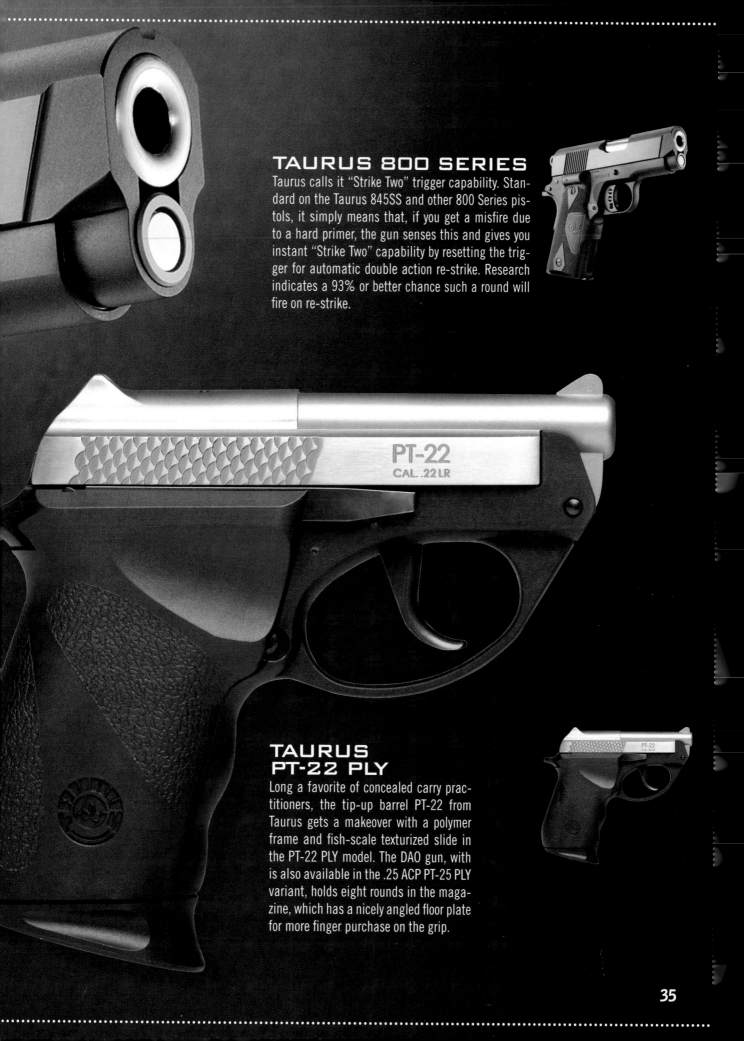

TAURUS 800 SERIES

Taurus calls it "Strike Two" trigger capability. Standard on the Taurus 845SS and other 800 Series pistols, it simply means that, if you get a misfire due to a hard primer, the gun senses this and gives you instant "Strike Two" capability by resetting the trigger for automatic double action re-strike. Research indicates a 93% or better chance such a round will fire on re-strike.

TAURUS PT-22 PLY

Long a favorite of concealed carry practitioners, the tip-up barrel PT-22 from Taurus gets a makeover with a polymer frame and fish-scale texturized slide in the PT-22 PLY model. The DAO gun, with is also available in the .25 ACP PT-25 PLY variant, holds eight rounds in the magazine, which has a nicely angled floor plate for more finger purchase on the grip.

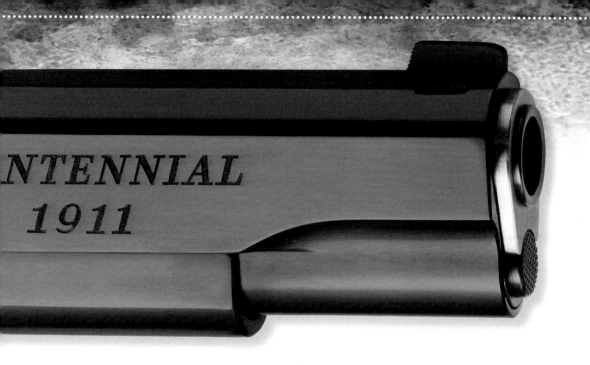

LES BAER CENTENNIAL

Les Baer Custom designed the Centennial as a fitting, 100-year tribute to the anniversary of John Browning's 1911 masterpiece. The special model has the appearance of a true collectible, including genuine ivory grips, which are a real rarity in this day and age.

LES BAER BOSS 1911

Inspiration can come from anywhere. In the case of this gun, Les Baer drew his from his favorite 1970s muscle car, the Boss 429 Mustang, a powerhouse Les admires above all other cars. As with other Baer pistols, the new Boss is guaranteed to shoot three-inch groups at 50 yards.

PARA BLACK OPS

The PARA Black Ops 14-45 pistol features a new, all-black IonBond finish, which is non-reflective and extremely durable. A high capacity .45 ACP pistol at 14+1 rounds, it comes with fixed combat-type night sights and an integral light rail

BERSA BP CC 9

The Bersa BP CC 9 is not unlike other lightweight (21.5 ounces) polymer pistols on the market. What makes it unique is its single-stack mag design and thin profile. Holding 8+1 rounds of 9mm, and with a 3.3-inch barrel, this ergonomic pistol is designed with comfort in mind for the person who carries concealed.

SPHINX
SDP COMPACT

The new Sphinx SDP Compact 9x19mm Parabellum is a compact Double-Action/Single-Action, with an ambidextrous decocking lever and mag catch. The gun's frame is unique in that the upper frame or dust cover is made from aeronautic-grade, hard-anodized aluminum with Teflon inserts to reduce wear.

CAL 380

COLT'S PT. FA., MFG. CO.
HARTFORD, CT. U.S.A.

COLT

COLT .380 MUSTANG

Like many of the handguns in Colt's lineup, the .380 ACP Mustang Pocketlite come and go. No doubt reintroduced to meet the growing demand for thin, light concealed carry guns, Colt's lovers will be glad this trim little, 12.5-ounce pistol is once again rolling off the factory assembly line.

WALTHER PPK/S

This fabulous little Walther PPK/S features factory engraving throughout its stainless steel slide, frame, and grips. It is chambered for .380 ACP. The Walther became known to millions on the silver screen in the James Bond "007" movies, but you don't have to be a secret agent to enjoy this pistol for gun collecting or concealed carry.

GLOCK GEN4

In its quest for perfection and world domination of the handgun market, Glock's **Gen4** pistols offer refinements over earlier designs, such as the addition of the Multiple Back Strap (MBS) system, which allows each user to tailor the grip to their own hand size.

CZ 75 SHADOW

The CZ custom shop has tuned up this pistol for any-one interested in competing or who wants to do some serious paper punching, with a finely tuned double-action/single action and a slide that is absent a firing pin block, a feature that greatly improves the already silky target trigger pull.

CZ P-07

The most unique feature of the tough-looking OD Green CZ P-07 duty is the Omega trigger system, which simplifies the CZ 75 trigger by using fewer parts for an improved trigger pull and easier maintenance. The Omega system also allows you to choose between operating the handgun with a decocking lever (installed) or a manual safety (included) via a simple parts exchange.

RUGER · PRESCOTT, AZ USA   SR22P   22LR

SR22 PISTOL

READ INSTRUCTION MANUAL BEFORE USING FIREARM

RUGER SR22

This lightweight (17.5 ounces) pistol chambered in .22 LR is a swell plinker for tearing up paper or for small-game hunting. New to Ruger's line up, it comes with two different size grips - Slim or Wider Palm Swell - to make what is already an ergonomic design even better. The sights are a high visibility white dot fixed on the front and the rear is adjustable. It even has a front end built-in Picatinny rail for accessories.

ROHRBAUGH R9

Sometimes it's best to start small—and stay that way. As in the R9 pistols from New York company Rohrbaugh Firearms. In both a Standard (top photo) and Stealth variant, these two pistols are perhaps the tiniest 9mms available for the serious carry practitioner. Without a sharp edge in sight, their profile minimizes the risk of the gun printing through clothing—and that is essential to the concealed part of concealed carry. Of course, at just 13.5 ounces empty, you may have to remind yourself you're carrying one of these little gems at all. The Standard model boasts a stainless finish slide, while the Stealth gets a friction-reducing black nitride finish. Otherwise identical, either are available with or without sights.

DAN WESSON ECO

The Dan Wesson ECO is a true single-stack, officer's-size 1911, weighing in at only 25 ounces. The gun wears Tritium night sights with a tactical ledge sight, and the ECO barrel is a flush-cut ramped bull barrel with target crown, rather than the traditional barrel and barrel bushing. This makes the gun slightly more compact and also easier to disassemble.

HECKLER & KOCH HK45

The HK45 Compact Tactical is the civilian version of the M24 handgun carried by the U.S. Navy Seals, and was developed as a slimmed down version of the full-size HK45, which in turn was created as an improvement to the popular, but square and bulky USP45 the company began offering back in the late 1990s. Following the custom fit trend across nearly all major manufacturers, this pistol comes standard with replaceable grip panels to adjust the feel and via circumference alteration. Available in double-action/single-action or a double-action-only model with an LEM (Law Enforcement Modification) trigger system, this gun comes equipped with an eight-round magazine, but readily accepts the 10-rounders from the full-size model. Controls are totally ambidextrous, and the magazine release gets supersized for a virtually no-miss hit when you need it most. Oh, and don't worry about shooting the life out of this gun. Heckler & Koch's polygonal rifling lengthens barrel life while increasing accuracy at the same time, which means there's no excuse for lots of range time with this one. After all, there's no real need for concern regarding the gun's longevity, plus you should know that the H&K proprietary internal mechanical recoil reduction system reduces the recoil forces affecting the weapon and shooter by as much as 30 percent. Now if all this doesn't encourage you to get out and shoot one of these wonderguns, we don't know what will.

KIMBER SUPER CARRY ULTRA

Kimber makes a dizzying array of 1911 variations, and you can't want just one. The Super Carry Ultra (the left pistol in the large photo), though, should top the list for those looking for a personal-defense gun. We love the fish-scale "serrations" at the slide and front strap, and the rounded heel of the backstrap increases the comfort level while carrying. Add in night sights, a shorty 3-inch barrel and rounded, snag-free edges, and this is a carry winner bar none. But you say you want something more? Okay, then simply contact the Custom Shop for a wider selection of options and end up with a beauty like the gun to the right.

KIMBER CLASSIC CARRY PRO

Created in the Kimber Custom Shop, the new Classic Carry Pro .45 ACP is a spectacular pistol. This "classy performance" carry pistol has a deep charcoal blue finish from Turnbull Restoration, complemented by bone grips. The steel frame and slide combine with a 4-inch bushing-less match grade bull barrel for perfect balance.

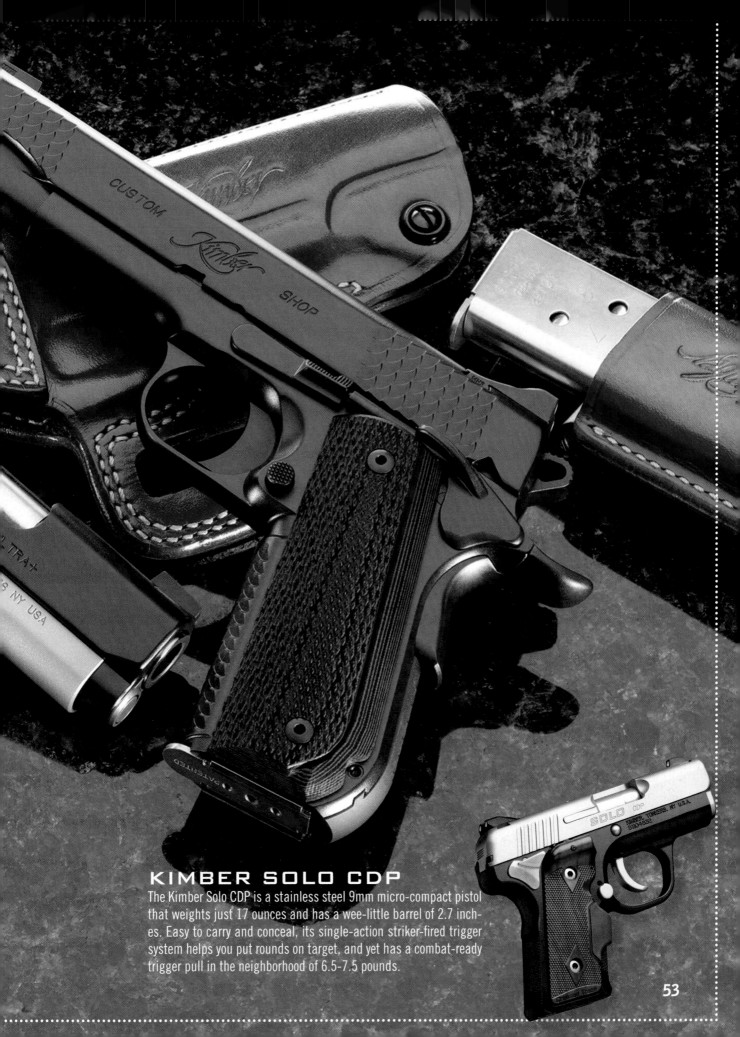

KIMBER SOLO CDP

The Kimber Solo CDP is a stainless steel 9mm micro-compact pistol that weights just 17 ounces and has a wee-little barrel of 2.7 inches. Easy to carry and conceal, its single-action striker-fired trigger system helps you put rounds on target, and yet has a combat-ready trigger pull in the neighborhood of 6.5-7.5 pounds.

45 AUTO Ⓡ

RUGER
PRESCOTT, AZ USA

664-68078

RUGER

BEFORE USING GUN-READ WARNINGS IN *INSTRUCTION M...*
FROM STURM, RUGER AND CO., INC. PRESCO...

RUGER

RUGER KP345

Ruger's semi-auto centerfire pistols have earned a reputation over the decades for solid dependability. Still, they never won a ton of awards in the looks department. But the new KP345 shows a marked improvement in cosmetics, with a less-chunky grip than its forebears, and useful accessories like the under-barrel accessory mount and ambidextrous slide-mounted manual safety/decocker. All around, a nice .45 ACP that should last its owner a lifetime.

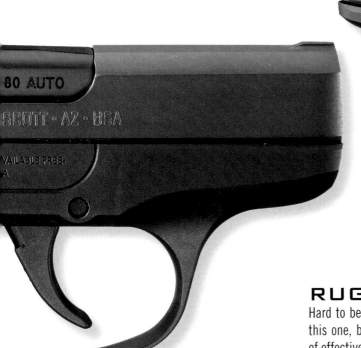

RUGER LCP .380

Hard to believe you can get a centerfire pistol as small as this one, but Ruger's miniscule LCP .380 ACP is a wonder of effective miniaturization. In four variations, two of which include either a LaserMax Centerfire or Crimson Trace Laserguard laser, the "heaviest" of these little powerhouses weighs a flat 10 ounces. Yet this is no Saturday Night Special. With a high-performance glass-filled nylon frame, this one can take a beating in a street fight that gets down and dirty. If the LCP is maybe too small for you, though, then step up a skimpy seven ounces to the 9mm LC9 model. Both laser options are available on this model, as well, plus there's an adjustable three-dot sight version.

RUGER SR9C

When capacity is your feature of choice, look no further than the SR9C Compact 9mm from Ruger. The long, nicely contoured grip on this full-size pistol holds a stellar 17 rounds. Striker-fired for a manageable double-action-only pull, this pistol also has a reversible backstrap for grip fit tailoring, a front frame accessory mount, and both an ambi- mag release button and decocker.

WALTHER P22

Walther keeps novices and experts on target with the P22, which features interchange-able backstraps, front sights, and barrels. The .22 LR pistol is a true double-action and features ambidextrous controls.

WALTHER SP22

Totally modular, dude! That's what the Wal-ther SP22 is, thanks to the .22 LR pistol's swap-out barrels, grip frames, sights, and Picatinny rails. Adjustable triggers and laser add-ons add icing to the cake.

RUGER SR1911

We're not sure if Ruger's the last manufacturer out there to put out a 1911, but it has one now, nonetheless. This nice .45 is no slouch, either, with CNC machining that generates tight tolerances and excellent slide-to-frame fit, and a barrel and bushing that are manufactured from a single bar of stainless steel stock, both on the same machine, a process that Ruger claims improves the gun's overall accuracy. Features like the diamond-pattern checkering on the nicely figured walnut grips, and a skeletonized trigger adjustable for overtravel, round out this classic iteration.

BERETTA BOBCAT

Tiny pistols have their place in self-defense, but their narrow slides are difficult to rack. Beretta solved the problem with a tip-up barrel in its pocket-sized Bobcats, available in both .22 LR and .32 ACP. Both operate by way of a direct blowback action. The sights are no-nonsense and low-profile for close-in work.

MOD. 21A-.22 LR MADE IN USA
BERETTA U.S.A. CORP. ACCOKEEK, MD

DAA340337

BERETTA U22 NEOS

In Greek, "Neos" means "new." The U22 Neos from Beretta is a modular pistol that has a neato-keen carbine kit available that makes this gun versatile across target disciplines and small-game hunting applications.

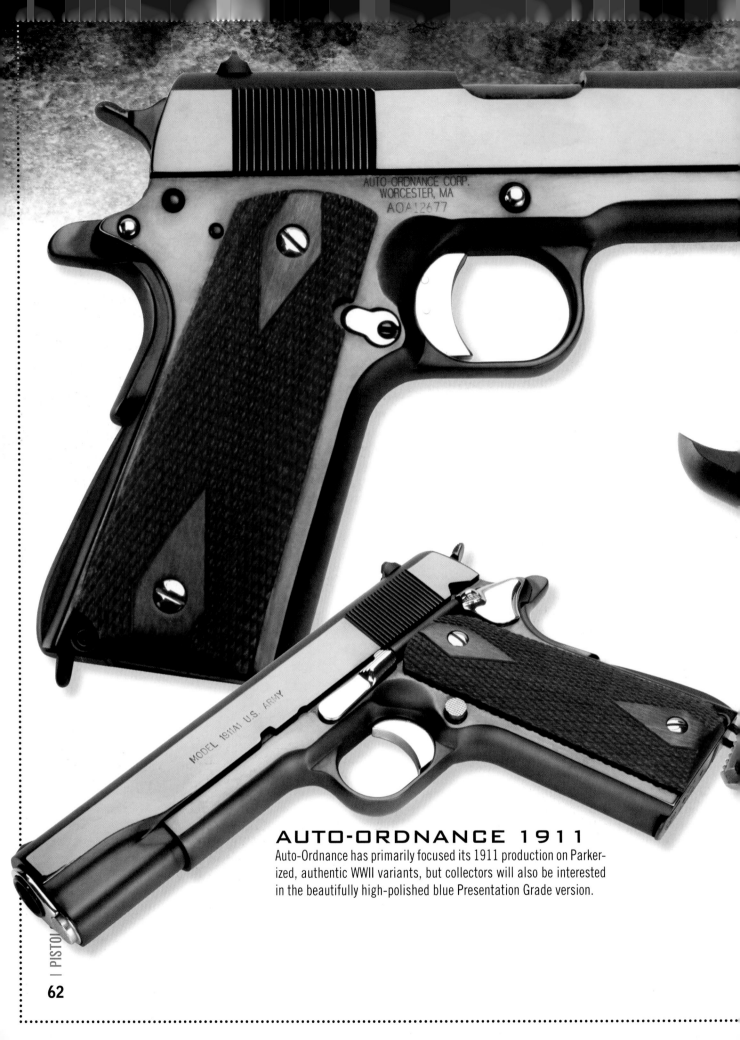

AUTO-ORDNANCE CORP.
WORCESTER, MA
AOA12677

MODEL 1911A1 U.S. ARMY

AUTO-ORDNANCE 1911

Auto-Ordnance has primarily focused its 1911 production on Parkerized, authentic WWII variants, but collectors will also be interested in the beautifully high-polished blue Presentation Grade version.

PARA WARTHOG

Most compact .45s have limited 6 or 7+1 capacities. If you want more, or even if you just have a bigger hand that appreciates a thicker grip, then Para USA's 14+1 Warthog is your carry gun.

KIMBER PRO AEGIS II

For those who find a full-size 1911-style pistol too big in the hand, the scaled down, slimmed down Pro Aegis II (above) from Kimber is an aluminum-framed 9mm that'll fit just right.

KIMBER CUSTOM COVERT II

Custom-shop built and loaded with features designed to make carry a breeze, Kimber's Custom Covert II (right) features night sights and built-in Crimson Trace laser grips. Plus you gotta totally dig the flat earth frame and desert camo combo!

KIMBER RIMFIRE
SUPER COMPETITION

The Kimber Rimfire Super Competition is for the super smallbore pistol champion, with features such as a lightweight aluminum frame, front strap and trigger guard checkering, and match-grade barrel and bushing.

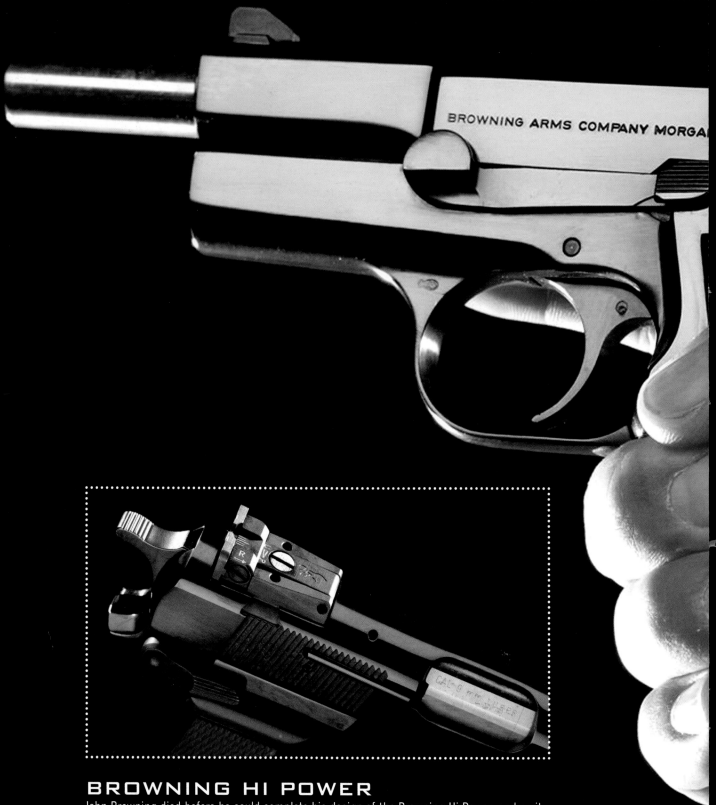

BROWNING HI POWER

John Browning died before he could complete his design of the Browning Hi Power, and so it was finished by Fabrique Nationale gunsmith Dieudonné Saive. In French, Hi Power is translated to "Grande Puissance," or GP, instead of our HP abbreviation.

COMBAT
★ELITE★

COLT ... CO. HARTFORD, CONN. U.S.A.

CG13487E

COLT COMBAT ELITE

Its name tells you that Colt's designed this gem for combat-sport shooters. To that end, speed-draw aficionados get a high-swept beavertail with a palm swell, a tactical safety lock, Colt's National Match barrel, and Novak sights. The single-action .45 ACP has a barrel, slide, and receiver of forged steel, and the gun also gets a full-length guide rod and improved hammer as additional enhancements.

COLT GOLD CUP

Introduced in the late 1950s, during the golden age of bull's-eye competition, Colt's Gold Cup is still the gold standard in out-of-the-box, match-ready 1911 pistols. The gun was originally introduced as the must-have pistol for competitors shooting in the sanctioned matches that originated in Caldwell, New Jersey, and which eventually migrated to week-long battle for bull's-eye domination at the NRA's Camp Perry National Matches. The Colt Gold Cup National Match is not to be confused with Colt's own National Match model, nor those National Match pistols of the same design produced by U.S. government armorers for U.S. Army Marksmanship unit shooters. Some of these latter guns can date back as far as the 1930s.

BERETTA 92FS/90-TWO

It took quite a gun to displace the venerable Colt 1911A1 Government as the military's primary sidearm. But the 9mm Beretta 92FS (above) did just that, unseating the single-action .45 ACP in 1985. The slightly modified version, the Model 90-Two, saw improved fit, function, and form over the original, including a subtle restyling effort, weight reduction, interchangeable wrap-around grips, and a MIL-STD-1913 accessory rail and rail cover..

BERETTA PX4 STORM SD

Beretta's Px4 Storm SD (Special Duty) has an edgy design that makes it look like it'll zip out of a holster as fast as the bullet will exit its muzzle—and that's sure to speed up your draw when you need it the most.

MAGNUM RESEARCH
MR EAGLE

Yes, Magnum Research does make guns for everyday use. Its MR "Fast Action" Pistol is based on Walther's P99 frame, making this 9mm or .40 S&W a super gun for the night stand, plinking, or speed shoots.

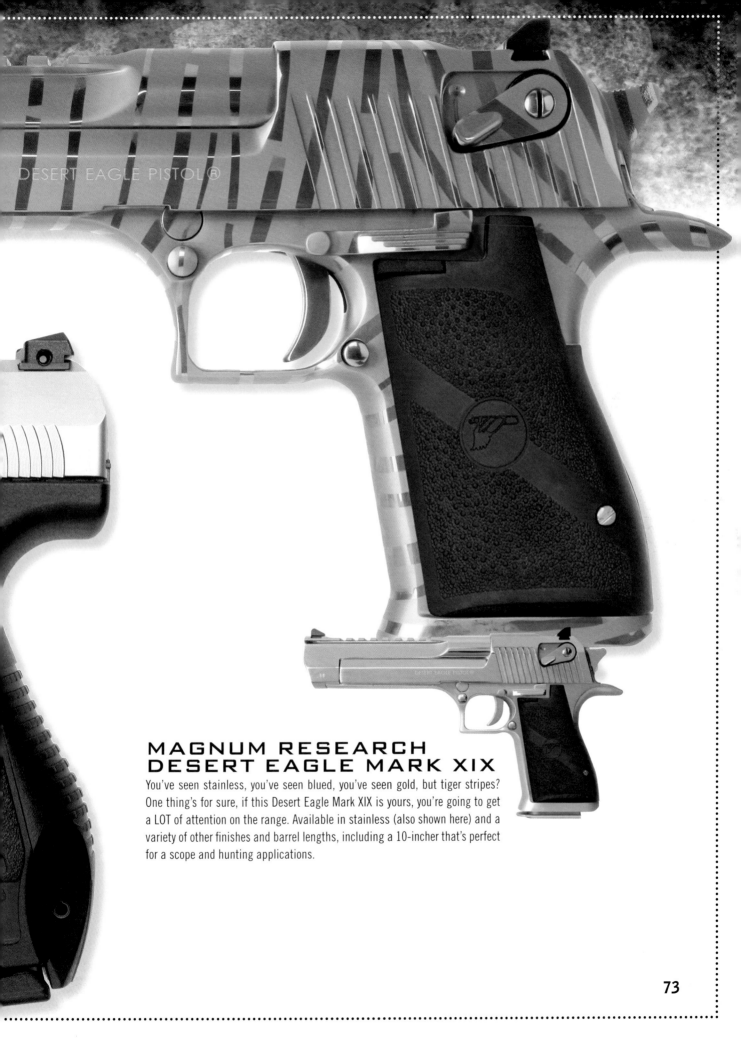

MAGNUM RESEARCH
DESERT EAGLE MARK XIX

You've seen stainless, you've seen blued, you've seen gold, but tiger stripes? One thing's for sure, if this Desert Eagle Mark XIX is yours, you're going to get a LOT of attention on the range. Available in stainless (also shown here) and a variety of other finishes and barrel lengths, including a 10-incher that's perfect for a scope and hunting applications.

KAHR ARMS
P380 BLACK ROSE

From purse to thigh holster to nightstand, the Kahr Arms P380 Black Rose is every woman's best friend. Super slim and super accurate, this .380 ACP is a terrific choice for any self-protection situation.

KAHR ARMS P380

Kahr Arms' superb pistols represent a strict dedication to concealed handgun perfection. Their lineup includes pocket holster gems such as the P380 polymer frame DAO, with night sights and a handy loaded chamber indicator.

KAHR ARMS TP9

The serrated front and back straps of the all-in-one polymer grip of Kahr's TP9 ensure a solid and reliable grip, whether you're drawing the gun out of a holster or taking it out of the night stand.

KIMBER TEAM MATCH II

From IDPA to IPSC to sanctioned bull's-eye and 3-gun matches, if you want to win, you need a gun that can take you to the top. Kimber's Team Match II, created for the USA Shooting Rapid Fire Pistol Team has every edge you need to squeeze everyone else on the line out of the running.

RUGER 22/45

A combination of a German 9mm Luger and a Colt Woodsman, Ruger's first .22 pistol was the gun that launched the company. Today's Threaded Barrel 22/45 is just one of many takes on the original, with Picatinny rails top and bottom and the ability to add all sorts of accessories.

CZ 2075 RAMI

The powerful .40 S&W round is right at home in the CZ's 2075 RAMI. The gun's short 3½-inch barrel is suitable for inside-the-waistband holsters and is also easily concealed under a sports coat in a shoulder rig.

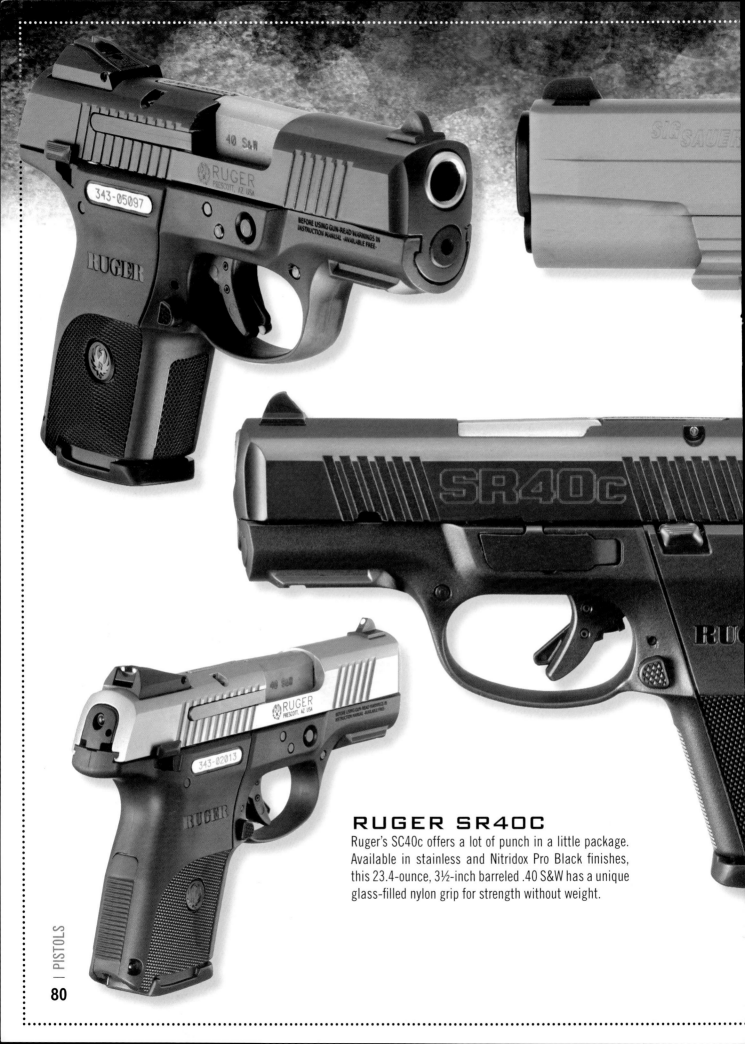

RUGER SR40C

Ruger's SC40c offers a lot of punch in a little package. Available in stainless and Nitridox Pro Black finishes, this 23.4-ounce, 3½-inch barreled .40 S&W has a unique glass-filled nylon grip for strength without weight.

SIG SAUER 1911 SCORPION

SIG Sauer shakes things up in the 1911 looks department with a desert tan Cerakote finish and Hogue's totally cool fish scale-textured Piranha Magwell Grip Set that incorporates the mainspring housing and an integrated mag well extension.

SIG SAUER P238

How much fun are these carry pistols from SIG?! The model P238, a trim and discreet single-stack .380 ACP single-action comes in a variety of off-the-wall frame colors and grip configurations. Who says your concealed gun has to be black? After all, it's *concealed*!

SIG SAUER MOSQUITO

The hot pink Mosquito from SIG Sauer is chambered in .22 LR and scaled to fit a smaller hands. While the audience aimed for with the screaming hot pink variant is certainly of the fairer gender, it's an excellent choice for getting women and young adults started in the shooting sports (and if you can't dig the pink, then the Multi-Cam version covers the other end of the aesthetic spectrum). SIG Sauer's Mosquito is a 90-percent scale version of the original, full-size 9mm P226. Standard equipment includes the integrated rail on the frame's underside for accessory mounting, as well as multiple safety features.

TAURUS 738 TCP

At just 10.2 ounces, you're never going to know you're carrying the Model 738 TCP from Taurus. This polymer-framed semi-auto holds 6+1 rounds of .380 ACP, and is the lightest pistol in the Taurus lineup.

TAURUS 1911

Yes, it's entirely possible to bling out your favorite gun. This custom shop Taurus PT 1911 AR gets high-contrast gold trigger, beavertail, hammer, and thumb safety on a bright stainless frame. Pearl grips give the gun even more luxury.

SIG SAUER P226 EQUINOX

The .40 S&W has all the accuracy and reliability you'd expect from a SIG Sauer gun, but the P226 Equinox gets its great looks—including a two-tone Nitron stainless slide and black hard-anodized alloy frame paired with nickel accents and gray laminated grips—from the craftsmen in SIG's custom shop.

TAURUS PT2011

Big power in a small package is what you get with the .40 S&W polymer-over-steel frame PT2011 from Taurus. It holds a whopping 11+1 rounds, but is only five inches high and 1.15 inches wide.

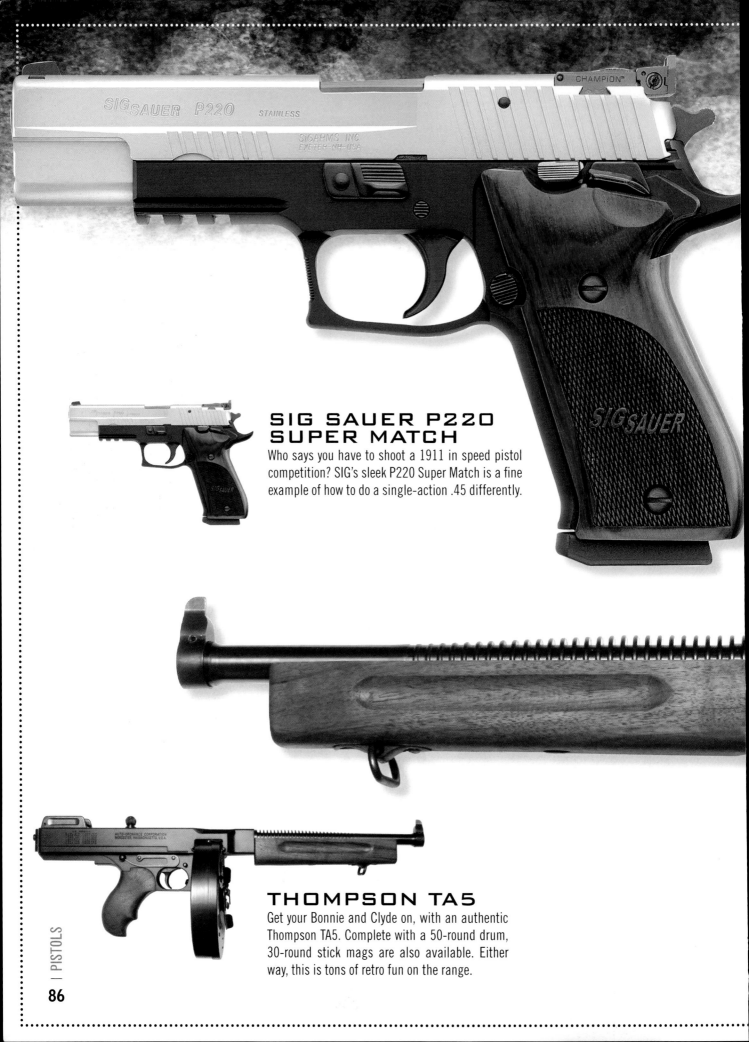

SIG SAUER P220 SUPER MATCH

Who says you have to shoot a 1911 in speed pistol competition? SIG's sleek P220 Super Match is a fine example of how to do a single-action .45 differently.

THOMPSON TA5

Get your Bonnie and Clyde on, with an authentic Thompson TA5. Complete with a 50-round drum, 30-round stick mags are also available. Either way, this is tons of retro fun on the range.

SIG SAUER P226 X5

If you love the fast pace and non-stop action of IPSC, IDPA, or 3-gun matches, then you're gonna want to holster SIG Sauer's P226 X5. Its cold hammer-forged barrel is beyond accurate, and the ergonomic grip is all it takes to stay steady in awkward shooting positions or when shooting weak-handed.

THOMPSON/CENTER CONTENDER

If you've always loved handguns and always loved putting venison in the freezer, then Thompson/Center's long-barreled stainless Contender in .30-30 is the right hunting gun for you.

COLT NEW AGENT

The words "double-action only" and "Colt" don't usually go together, but, when they do, they make a beautiful concealment pistol. With an anodized aluminum receiver and 3-inch barrel, the Colt New Agent DAO is great discreet and snag-free carry choice.

FNH USA FIVE-SEVEN

Chambering the low-recoil 5.7x28mm pistol round, the single-action Five-seveN semi-auto from FNH USA features a polymer slide cover that reduces weight, ambidextrous manual safety levers, and a reversible magazine release. The frame is ergonomically designed and boasts checkered panels, a big benefit on a polymer frame, especially when the action is hot and your hands are sweaty during summertime fun on the range. This rather unique pistol, one that is turning lots of heads, thanks to FNH USA's big sponsorships in the lava-hot game of 3-gun competition, also gets a hammer-forged and chrome-lined barrel, two features that increase accuracy and prolong barrel life. Sights are easily swappable and come in a variety of configurations, controls are ambidextrous, and the mag release is reversible. We also like that FNH USA offers the gun not only in the every day matte black, but also in the uber-cool olive drab and flat earth dressings. And, oh, did we mention? There's a whopping 20-round magazine available! Reload less, shoot more!

SPRINGFIELD ARMORY XD(M)

Did you know that the "M" in XD(M) stands for "More?" As in more features even in this wonderful little XD(M)-9 3.8 Compact version. There's an accessory rail, striker-status indicator, loaded chamber indicator, ambidextrous magazine release. Most unique to this size class and a polymer framed pistol is the grip safety. Combined with the waffled texture of the grip itself, a firm purchase is both necessary and enhanced, something that can only help you control this gun in a time of dire need.

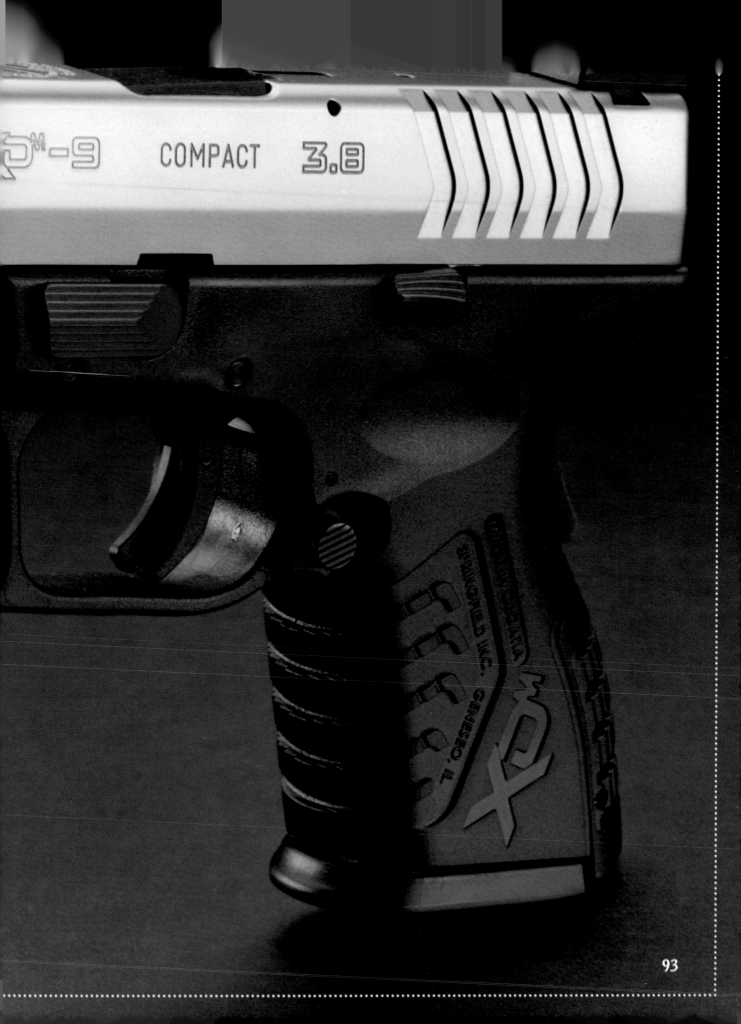

RHINO 20
357 MAGNUM cal. 18238
Chiappa Firearms, Dayton, OI
Made in Italy by KIMAR

REVOLVERS

Despite the firearms world moving towards one where the tactical semi-automatics and their rakish designs dominate, revolvers remain a tried and true choice for many shooting enthusiasts.

People choose revolvers for different reasons. For instructors and beginners, revolvers are a smart choice for a first handgun, since their function can be easily observed and understood—the cocking of the hammer, the rotation of the cylinder, the loaded chambers—it's all pretty simple stuff.

That simplicity is what makes revolvers attractive choices for other handgunners. They are easy to clean and maintain, and their durability and dependability is proven. Malfunctions are rare and, when they do occur, junk ammo is usually to blame, rather than the gun. These firearms are self-contained, so there's no worry of losing or dropping a magazine, as can happen with a semi-auto. Revolvers are also still the go-to choice for serious hunters looking to take big game with a handgun; indeed, autoloaders are rarely considered for such use. Finally, although the vast majority of law enforcement officers carry autoloaders these days, revolvers have the longest history of any type of firearm to be used in the line of duty day in and day out. The Smith & Wesson Model 586 featured here is one of them.

With the rise in the number of states approving concealed carry laws, many citizens are rushing to purchase handguns, and revolvers often become a choice for a personal-defense weapon. Some manufacturers are well known for their powerful, sturdy, snubnose revolvers that come in a wide variety of calibers. Too, there are some models of derringer-like "mini" revolvers made by North American Arms that could be concealed in a coffee cup, yet pack solid punch at close range. Many gunmakers are offering ultra-lightweight models for those who will carry their shooting piece on a daily basis. This trend in lightweight frames even extends to those spin-shooters chambering Magnum calibers, something that backpackers and hikers traveling in bear and mountain lion territory appreciate, as every ounce counts when you're carrying it all on your back.

Another trend in the revolver world is the still-growing sport of the amazingly popular cowboy action shooting, where the wheelguns rule the day. Most guns are based on the design of the Colt Single Action Army, the iconic pistol that won the West. This type of single-action revolver is still a popular choice for a person who wants a do-it-all pistol. From target shooting and competitions to hunting, self-defense, and plinking, some things never go out of style.

In the *Gun Digest Book of the Revolver*, author Grant Cunningham writes, "I've said for many years that the revolver is the easiest gun to shoot, but the hardest gun to shoot well. There is a personal satisfaction to shooting a revolver well, and it's magnified when you can do it to the point that you can beat people who insist on using those newfangled self-shucking things!"

—*James Card, Editor,* Gun Digest the Magazine

UBERTI NEW MODEL CATTLEMAN MATCHING SET

Uberti makes some of the finest Old West reproductions seen today. This matched and cased set of blued and case colored New Model Cattleman single-action revolvers have matched serial numbers differentiated only by an "L" or an "R" in indication of left- or right-hand use.

BERETTA STAMPEDE MARSHALL OLD WEST

Beretta's dedication to making the fine handguns reminiscent of times gone by shows itself well in the Stampede Marshall Old West. The 3½-inch barrel .45 LC is a delight to shoot and a nice departure from the vast array of SA Army replicas.

BERETTA
STAMPEDE DELUXE

The Beretta Stampede Deluxe features unbelievably deep charcoal bluing on the barrel and cylinder, while the frame is enhanced with Beretta Color-Case, which duplicates the romance of Old West color case hardening. It is a fine and exacting copy of a Colt Single Action Army, but one at a considerably lower price than a new one from today's Colt's factory.

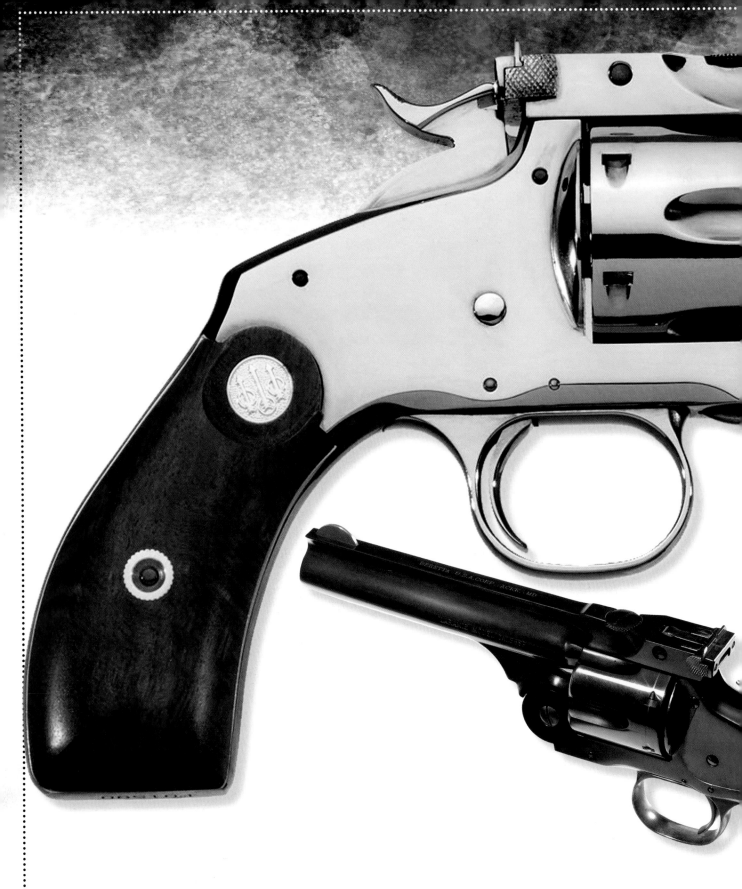

BERETTA LARAMIE

Offered for just a short time, the Beretta Laramie is a break-top revolver designed to appeal to cowboy action shooters. The six-shooter is available in both .45 LC and the gentler .38 Special. The gun featured an octagonal barrel, came in blue, nickel, and De Luxe versions, and was available in two barrel lengths, five and 6½ inches. A sliding bar safety was incorporated, a decided improvement over the revolver of yore it imitated, as this improvement allowed users to safely carry an all-chambers-loaded gun in the half-cock position.

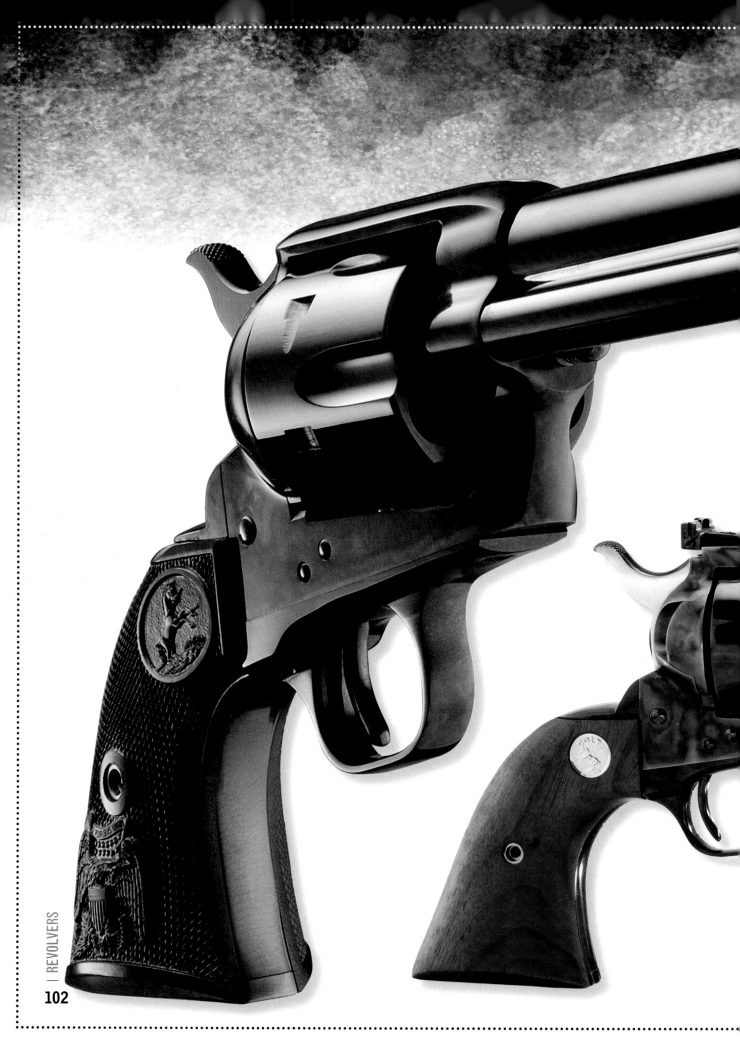

COLT NEW FRONTIER

With a barrel length of up to 7½ inches, the Colt New Frontier (below) is the target shooter's take on the company's original SAA, thanks to an adjustable rear sight and target ramped front sight. Colt's Royal blue finish on the barrel and cylinder complement the case colored frame. It is available in both .44 Special and .45 LC, either of which come stocked with walnut grips bearing the timeless Colt rearing horse logo in a gold medallion.

COLT SINGLE ACTION ARMY

The black composite eagle stocks on the newest version of the Single Action Army from Colt's keep this gun as Old West real as it ever was. This is the original of the original, replete with some of the deepest bluing and most vivid case coloring around. A high-polished nickel version is also available, and calibers other than the standard .45 LC can be optioned through Colt's custom shop.

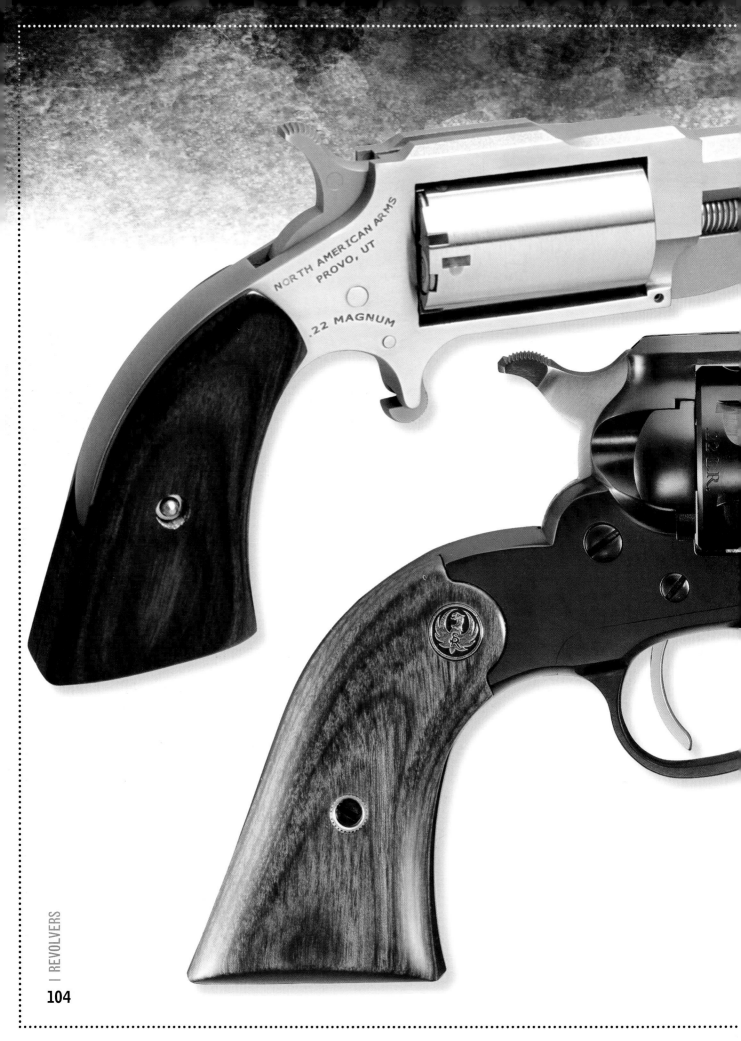

NORTH AMERICAN ARMS
PROVO, UT

.22 MAGNUM

NORTH AMERICAN ARMS 1860 HOGLEG

The North American Arms 1860 Hogleg is a five-shot, single-action, mini-revolver chambered in .22 Magnum. The pistol features a half-way notch cylinder that allows the hammer to rest on a loaded chamber without fear of accidental discharge. It has a fixed bead front sight and rosewood grips.

RUGER BEARCAT

The Ruger Bearcat is a single-action .22 LR revolver with a one-piece, six-shot cylinder frame. Compact and light, it was designed to be an easy-to-carry trail gun for general use in the outdoors—think snakes and other small, generally disagreeable creatures you might come across as you wander the great outdoors. It comes in a blued or satin stainless finish.

UBERTI TOP BREAK

The Uberti Top Break is based on the 1869 cavalry pistol design of Major George Schofield and used by Jessie James, John Wesley Hardin, and Wild Bill Hickok. The U.S. Army at one point purchased 3,000 of these models, but the Russian Czar of the time really loved them, buying 41,000 top breaks with a modified grip design, lanyard ring, and a distinctive trigger spur.

UBERTI BIRD'S HEAD

The Uberti Bird's Head is a Colt SAA-type revolver. Its name comes from the rounded grip that slightly resembles the head of a bird. The grip style was also previously used on Colt derringers, in the 1850s. The revolver comes in different barrel lengths and in .45 Colt or .357 Magnum calibers. It sports a color case hardened frame and steel backstrap and trigger guard.

UBERTI 1873 BUNTLINE TARGET

The Uberti 1873 Buntline Target is a .45-caliber single-action revolver with an 18-inch barrel, angled front target sight, and an adjustable, notched rear blade sight. As the story goes, Ned Buntline, a dime store novelist, gave Wyatt Earp and four other lawmen Colt Single Action Army revolvers with extra-long barrels, which then, naturally, became known as Buntline Specials.

NORTH AMERICAN ARMS
.22 MAGNUM HOLSTER GRIP

The North American Arms .22 Magnum Holster Grip, shown to the left, is a mini-revolver that fits into its own built-in holster. Simply unfold it to the open position, and the "holster" becomes the gun's grip. The five-shot revolver uses a half-way notch cylinder, so that the hammer can rest securely on a loaded chamber.

NORTH AMERICAN ARMS PUG

The North American Arms Pug, below, is a small and sturdy mini-revolver chambered in .22 Magnum. It is ideal for concealed carry, thanks to its ultra-short one-inch heavy barrel. It has a pebble-textured grip for a sure hold and comes with either white dot or tritium sights, the latter of which make this an excellent pocket gun for going about your business in the dark.

CIMARRON FIREARMS THUNDERER

Designed for horse-mounted competitors, Cimarron Firearms' Thunderer, in both standard and hogleg grip designs, has nearly full-coverage checkering on its hardwood grips. For competitors in the heat of a cowboy action match, this provides improved hand purchase and overall control, especially during hot summer shoots where sweaty palms reign.

RUGER SINGLE-TEN

Practicing with a .22-caliber version of bigger bore guns is a great way to refine shooting form without spending big ammo dollars. For SASS competitors, Ruger's Single-Ten is good and smart practice on the cheap, thanks to its Williams fiber optic sight and 10-shot cylinder. Reload less, shoot more.

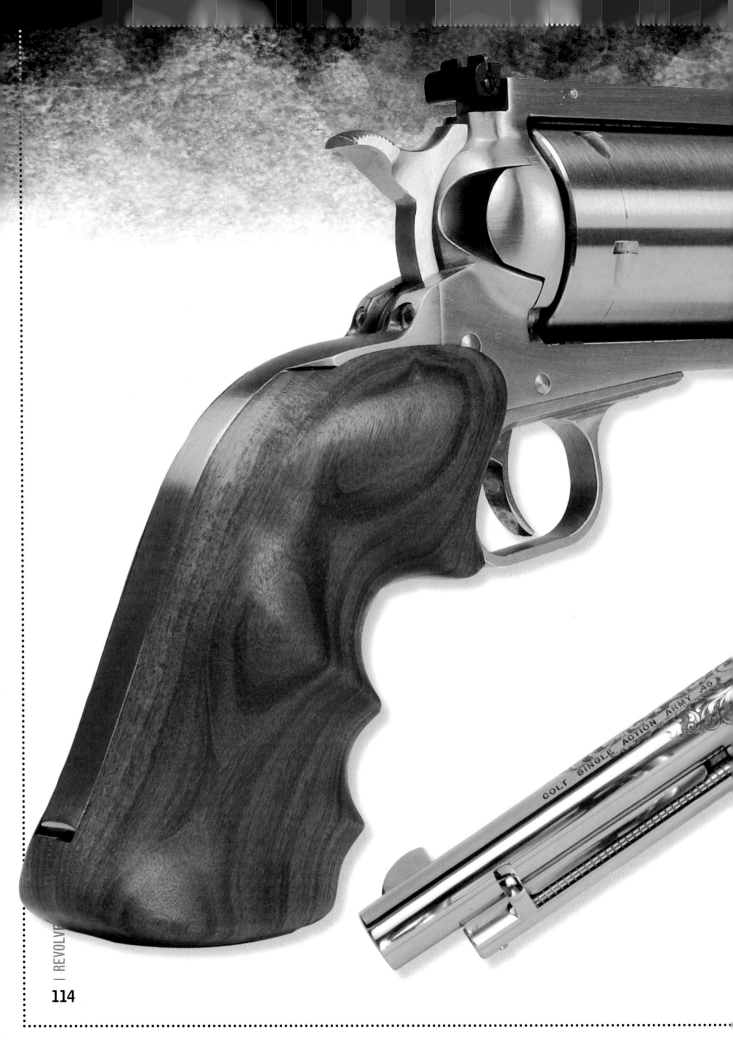

COLT SINGLE ACTION ARMY .45

MAGNUM RESEARCH BFR

If you just love big for big's sake, then you'll be nuts for Magnum Research's BFR, or Big Frame Revolver, or Big Fine Revolver, or Big You-Fill-In-The-Blank Revolver. This single-action giant houses your favorite overloads, such as the buffalo-worthy .45-70 and the grizzly ready .480 Ruger and .500 and .460 S&W Magnums. Magnum Research, part of the Kahr family of firearms, can also provide scope mounts and rings, HIVIZ fiber optic front sights in three height sizes, and several holster choices, including a bandolier rig that fits the 10-inch barrel BFRs.

COLT'S MODERN MASTERS

Owning a gun with a Colt's logo is owning a small piece of history, but never more so than when you add one as a true collectible to your gun vault. Today's Modern Masters Single Action Army revolvers are limited edition works of art, with refined hand engraving by Colt's two master engravers, Steve Kamyk and George Spring. Their art is ink-baked to add depth and character. Kamyk and Spring can cover up to 50 percent of an SAA, and, to ice the cake, the guns get a one-piece ivory grip (and notice we did not say ivory "look alike").

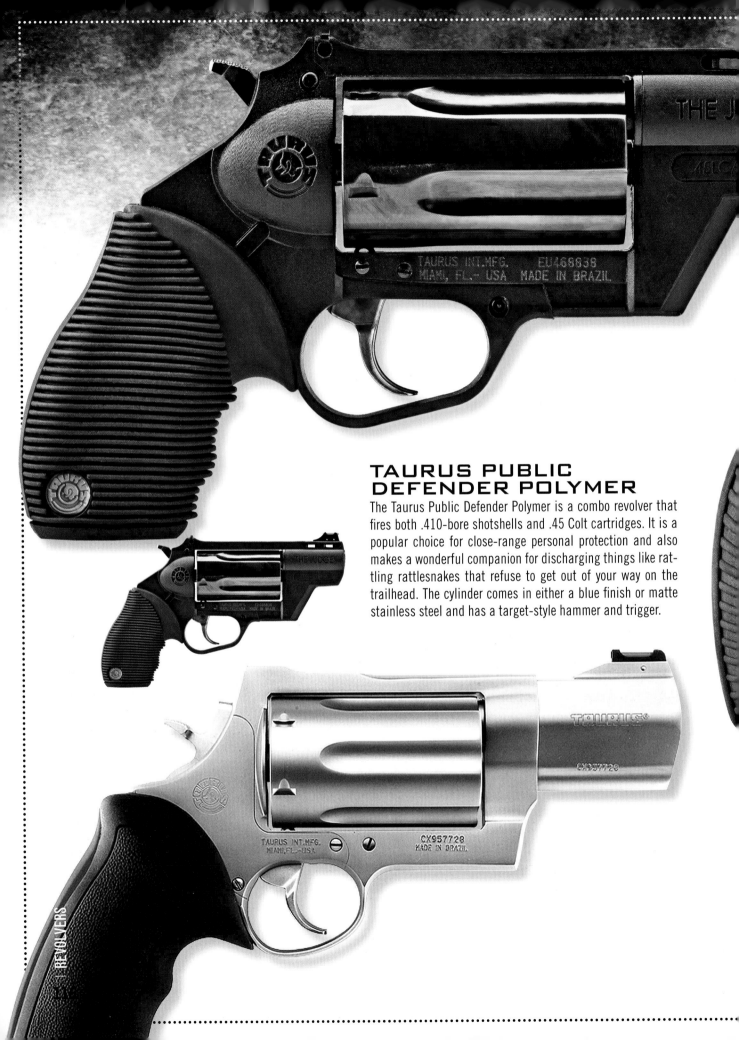

TAURUS PUBLIC DEFENDER POLYMER

The Taurus Public Defender Polymer is a combo revolver that fires both .410-bore shotshells and .45 Colt cartridges. It is a popular choice for close-range personal protection and also makes a wonderful companion for discharging things like rattling rattlesnakes that refuse to get out of your way on the trailhead. The cylinder comes in either a blue finish or matte stainless steel and has a target-style hammer and trigger.

TAURUS DT .357 MAGNUM REVOLVER

The new Taurus DT .357 Magnum Revolver has a lightweight polymer body frame and a clockwise cylinder rotation for fast loading. Once available in a matte finished frame paired with a high-polish blued cylinder, the cylinder and crane now also available in a contrasting matte stainless finish. Cushy ribbed rubber grips help you hang on to this one when firing full .357 Magnum loads.

TAURUS RAGING JUDGE MAGNUM

The Taurus Raging Judge Magnum covers the gamut, firing your choice of .454 Casull, the .45 Colt, and .410 3-inch shotshells from its six-round cylinder. It is available in 3-inch and 6½-inch barrels, and a cushion is built into the grip to reduce felt recoil—something you'll undoubtedly appreciate if you load this one up with the .454 Casull.

CHARTER ARMS CHIC LADY

The Charter Arms Chic Lady comes with a pink anodized frame and high-polished barrel, cylinder, crane, cylinder release, hammer, and trigger guard. This super-girly gun is just one of many in Charter's line-up of colored revolvers, which are a fun departure from the bazillions of blued and stainless guns out there. Constructed out of aircraft-grade aluminum and steel, the pistol weighs just 12 ounces.

RUGER SUPER REDHAWK

The Ruger Super Redhawk double-action revolver chambered for the .454 Casull pulls double duty with the .45 Colt cartridge, while the same gun chambered in .44 Magnum naturally fires the shorter-cased and milder .44 Special cartridges. It has a cushioned grip system to absorb the heavy recoil of these big-bore rounds, and a cylinder that triple locks at the front, rear, and bottom of the frame for greater dependability. The Super Redhawk 2½-inch barreled Alaskan version in either chambering (it has also been available in .480 Ruger, shown here) is an excellent inclusion in your survival kit, if you hike and hunt in places where you're not at the top of the food chain.

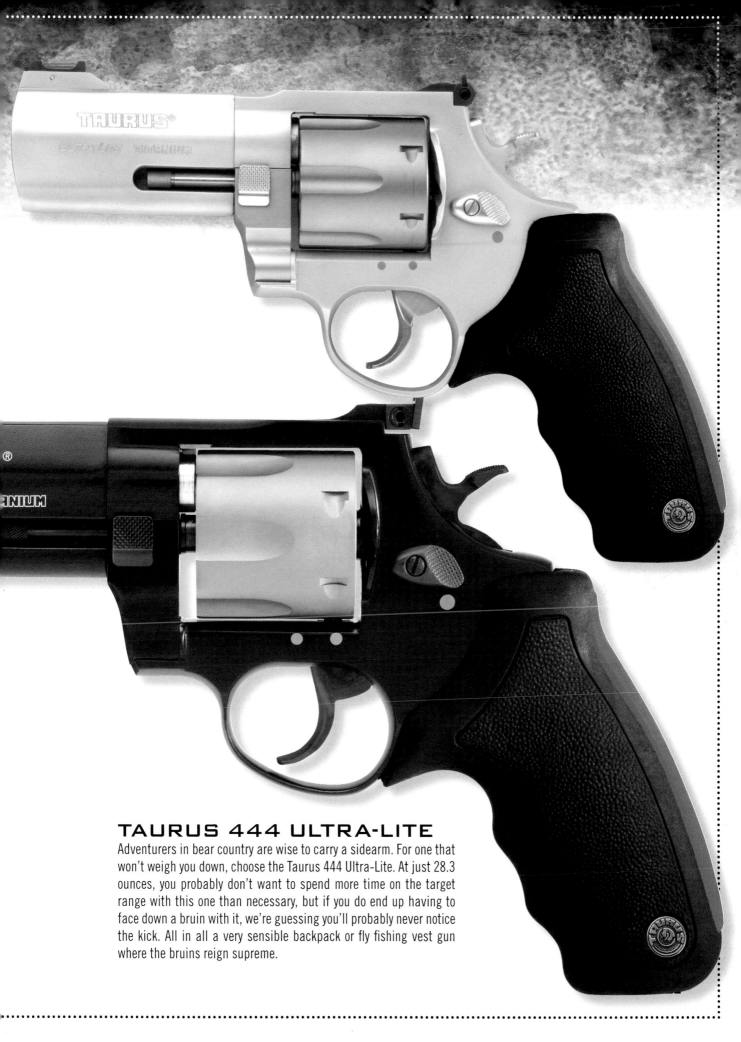

TAURUS 444 ULTRA-LITE

Adventurers in bear country are wise to carry a sidearm. For one that won't weigh you down, choose the Taurus 444 Ultra-Lite. At just 28.3 ounces, you probably don't want to spend more time on the target range with this one than necessary, but if you do end up having to face down a bruin with it, we're guessing you'll probably never notice the kick. All in all a very sensible backpack or fly fishing vest gun where the bruins reign supreme.

RUGER SP101

Ruger's triple-locking cylinder design nearly guarantees the SP101 is never out of timing. Today's variants include windage adjustable sights paired with a .327 Fed. Mag. chambering, along with the traditional grooved "no-sight" rear sight in .38 Special, .357 Magnum, and .22 LR.

SMITH & WESSON CHAMPION 625

Smith & Wesson took lessons from its own team shooting champions to create new guns. The Champion 625 in .45 ACP is the brainchild of Jerry Miculek—currently lending his star shooting power to the red hot sport of 3-gun—who has a list of revolver titles and speed shooting records as long as a June summer day in Alaska.

SMITH & WESSON GOVERNOR

Smith & Wesson jumped into the .410-bore revolver trend, with its long-cylinder Governor model. The six-rounder has a lightweight frame of scandium alloy, but is completely capable of handling the .45 LC and .45 ACP rounds that are, without question, stouter than a .410-bore shotshell. S&W clearly intends this gun for personal-defense, including a tritium night sight dovetailed into the muzzle end of the rib and optioning Crimson Trace laser grips. Moon clips are included with the gun so that users can use any and all combinations of handgun and shotshell ammunitions.

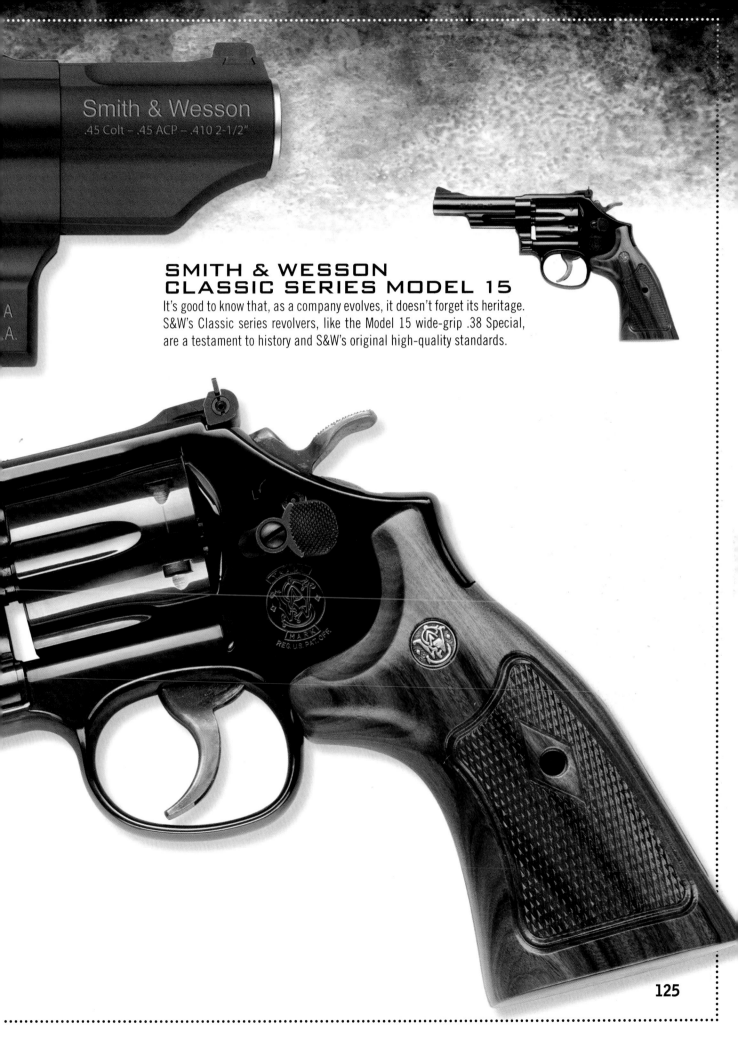

Smith & Wesson
.45 Colt – .45 ACP – .410 2-1/2"

SMITH & WESSON
CLASSIC SERIES MODEL 15

It's good to know that, as a company evolves, it doesn't forget its heritage.
S&W's Classic series revolvers, like the Model 15 wide-grip .38 Special,
are a testament to history and S&W's original high-quality standards.

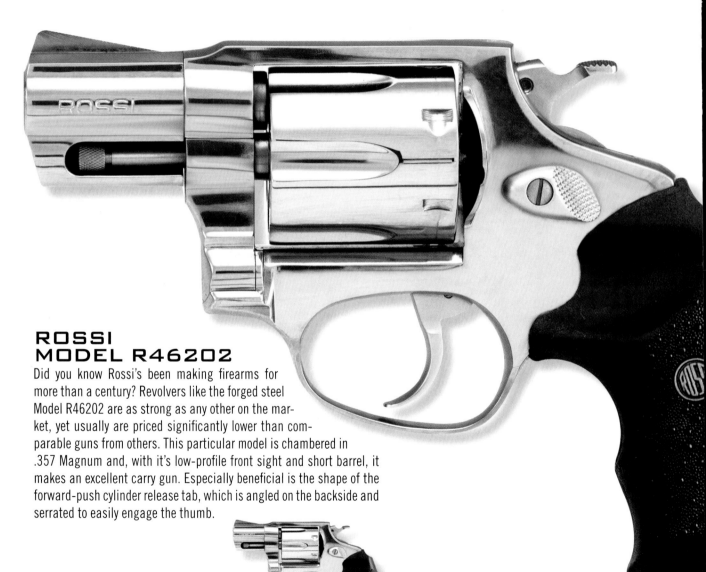

ROSSI
MODEL R46202

Did you know Rossi's been making firearms for more than a century? Revolvers like the forged steel Model R46202 are as strong as any other on the market, yet usually are priced significantly lower than comparable guns from others. This particular model is chambered in .357 Magnum and, with it's low-profile front sight and short barrel, it makes an excellent carry gun. Especially beneficial is the shape of the forward-push cylinder release tab, which is angled on the backside and serrated to easily engage the thumb.

SMITH & WESSON CLASSIC MODEL 586

The Smith & Wesson Classic Model 586 is a retro-styled revolver modeled after the old school Model 586, a handgun favored by decades of law enforcement officers. Chambered for .357 Magnum and, of course, its shorter .38 Special brother, the double-action revolver has a carbon steel frame and cylinder with a blue finish. It is available with 4- or 6-inch barrels.

ROSSI MODEL 851

The Rossi .38 Special +P Model 851 has a 4-inch vent rib barrel and six-round cylinder. It has adjustable rear sights and red inserts with elevated front sights. Complete with a lifetime repair policy, this revolver also includes the patented Taurus Security System (Taurus is Rossi's parent company) for an extra measure of safety.

ROSSI MODEL 972

The Rossi .357 Magnum Model 972 has a stainless steel 6-inch barrel. Deep-contour finger groups help maintain a sure grip with stiff loads, and the adjustable rear sight keeps you on target.

CHARTER ARMS PITBULL

The Charter Arms Pitbull is the world's first true *rimless* center-fire revolver—no moon clips are needed. This ground-breaking revolver is specifically chambered in .40-caliber, so it can be used as a back-up gun for those who carry a .40 S&W autoloader. It has a 2.3-inch barrel and five-shot capacity. A dual coil spring assembly in the extractor allows cartridges to be inserted and held in place in each chamber in the revolver cylinder.

RUGER NEW MODEL BLACKHAWK

The Ruger New Model Blackhawk is a single-action revolver with an all-coil spring mechanism, adjustable sights, and frame-mounted firing pin. The pistol comes in a wide variety of barrel lengths and includes chamberings for .30 Carbine, .357 Magnum, .41 Magnum, .44 Special, and .45 Colt.

CHARTER ARMS
DIXIE DERRINGER

The Dixie Derringer from Charter Arms is chambered in .22 Magnum. The single-action revolver holds five rounds, and, weighing in at just six ounces, it is a quick-draw pocket gun useful for concealed carry and close-range shooting.

CHARTER ARMS SNUBBY

Charter Arms makes dozens of snubby revolvers in a breathtaking array of colors. Pictured here are just a few imaginative choices, including the Lavender Lady, a choice of mottled pink or earth tones, bright turquoise, and a cool burgundy.

SPORTING RIFLES

What can you say about today's sporting rifles that hasn't been said before? For one, you can say it's nearly impossible to find a bad gun from any of the dozens of recognizable names out there. Even those in the bottom rungs of the pricing tiers get the job done, maybe not with great style, but certainly with accuracy. Indeed, the number of guns that shoot MOA or tighter these days are legion. This kind of accuracy used to be the domain of benchrest shooters, NRA High Power competitors, and handloading tweakers, you know, those accuracy "nuts." Now, it's nearly a given that the average Joe can buy whatever rifle he wants off the shelf, slap a decent scope on it (where again, even the cheap seats are nothing to sneeze at anymore), grab a box or two of ammo, and have the gun sighted in with little effort.

It's pleasing to see this kind of craftsmanship available to the masses, because it's something you used to have to pay dearly for. In fact, it's as if the gun manufacturers have come to see the light surrounding accuracy the way car manufacturers came around to safety issues. Name me a modern production vehicle, even the cheapest, no-frills, roll-down window model that doesn't come with air bags and anti-lock brakes—can't do it, can you? The theory with the cars, I'd go out on a limb to say, was that safety shouldn't be a privilege. Same goes with guns and accuracy. Accuracy just shouldn't be a privilege.

As good as today's centerfires are—and they are very good—some will consider the genre of rimfires even better. For generations, a .22 rifle has been the first gun for many young shooters, a rite of passage to adulthood. This continues to be a fact of life in some areas, but changing lifestyles make this kind of upbringing less common today, since most youngsters are growing up in urban areas, where finding a place to shoot is difficult or impossible. Still, whether you grow up in an area where guns are part of daily life, or a youngster is merely fortunate enough to have a parent, older brother, or some other mentor who can properly introduce them to the world of shooting, very likely that intro would involve a .22 rifle.

As a tool for introducing youngsters to shooting is only a small part of the rimfire segment of the firearms industry. Many adults buy and use rifles chambered for the "lowly" little .22, which has been around in one form or another for 125 years and is considered to be the most popular cartridge in the entire world. There are several reasons for this continued popularity of rimfires.

In a soft economy, the cost of buying and shooting a rimfire is less—sometimes much less—than a centerfire. For well under $400 or $500, you can pick up a well-made .22- or .17-caliber rifle (or even a handgun) that can give years of fun, whether it's used for practice, plinking, or hunting. Too, the price of rimfire ammunition is a fraction of what it is for centerfire cartridges. It's not hard to find 500-round boxes of LR for under $200, less than four cents a pop.

It should be remembered that the term "rimfire" isn't restricted to .22-caliber rifles or ammo. In today's world, there are a couple .17-caliber rimfire rounds, and several sub-caliber wildcats in .10-, .12-, and .14-caliber can be had in custom rifles. And then there is the .22 Winchester Magnum Rimfire (WMR). Ammo for the .22 WMR, the .17 HMR, and .17 Mach 2 is a bit more expensive than the standard .22, but still a lot less than centerfire prices.

Other reasons for the continued popularity of rimfires are the very obvious ones, the lack of recoil and relatively quiet report. A few hours at the shooting bench with a rimfire are a piece of cake, when compared to that same time spent with most centerfires. This makes the rimfire ideal for teaching beginners the shooting basics. The lack of a loud report and muzzle blast also help a beginner learn trigger control without developing a flinch.

The firearms industry has been very aggressive in producing rimfire versions of centerfire rifles in recent years, especially in the tactical gun category. Almost every rifle manufacturer today offers at least one AR-type rifle, and several are marketing uppers to allow shooters to turn their .223/5.56mm into a rimfire.

The rimfire rifle part of the firearms world is alive and well. One could say that the millions of rimfire rifles already in the hands of American shooters might beg the question, "Do we really need more?" We say the key word there is "need." To most of us, the whole idea of our hobby is to find a reason to have more guns, not less!

—*Jennifer L.S. Pearsall, Editor Gun Digest Books, and*
Jerry Lee, Editor at Large Gun Digest Books

MOSSBERG 715T FLAT TOP

The 715 Flat Top is a new version of the tactical Mossberg .22 rifle that was introduced in 2010 and is based on the Model 702 Plinkster action. Without the carry handle of the first model, the Tactical Flat Top has a full-length Picatinny top rail. Other features include a free-floating 16¼-inch barrel, removable front and rear adjustable sights, and an ergonomic pistol grip. There is a choice of adjustable or fixed stock in matte black or camo finish, and a Picatinny quad rail fore-end. Another option is the combo version with a 30mm red dot sight.

MOSSBERG 464

Most lever-action rifles are very traditional in appearance and based on nineteenth century designs—and, frankly, they all look alike. Not so with the Mossberg 464 SPX. While it operates like a lever-action and has all the pluses shooters have come to expect with this type of rifle—they are reliable, accurate, and fast-handling—the 464 SPX is also a tactical-style rifle with features like a six-position adjustable stock, accessory rails, adjustable fiber optic sights, and an optional flash suppressor and muzzle brake. This latest Mossberg rimfire has a machined receiver with a properly positioned ejection port that works with receiver-mounted optics. It is also available in .30-30 Winchester.

BROWNING BUCK MARK TARGET RIFLE

Take a Browning Buck Mark pistol, put a long heavy barrel on it, and attach a buttstock to its backstrap with a skeletonized brace and whaddaya get? Browning's Buck Mark Target Rifle. One of the most unique-looking .22 rifles on the market ever made.

BROWNING T-BOLT STAINLESS SPORTER SPORTING RIFLE

Browning scores all sorts of points in the "different" category, with its T-Bolt Stainless Sporter. In .22 LR, .22 WMR or .17 HMR, the straight-pull bolt is an uncomplicated and efficient design on this field-worthy small-game gun.

COOPER MODEL 57-M

Cooper Arms of Montana has been making fine bolt-action and single-shot centerfire rifles since 1990. In 2000, the rimfire Model 57 was added to the company's lineup. It was originally offered in .22 LR and .22 WMR, and when the .17 HRM round was introduced, in 2002, it, too, was added to the list. Made to match the company's centerfire rifles, the Model 57-M is offered in several variations with an oil-finished, hand-checkered AA Claro walnut stock, 22- or 24-inch barrels in blue or stainless, and quality workmanship all the way around. You won't find a nicer bolt-action .22 currently in production in the U.S.A.

MARLIN XT-17VLB
Shoot the hottest rimfire around with out-and-out precision in Marlin's XT-17VLB. With a funky-cool laminated thumb-hole stock, the .17HMR is hours of paper punching or small varmint hunting fun.

BROWNING SA-22
More than a few gun writers have referred to Browning's SA-22 as the most beautiful .22 ever made. This svelte 5¼-pound legend goes all the way back to the man himself, John Moses Browning, the greatest gun inventor who ever lived. The original design was sold by Browning to Remington and was made as the Remington Model 24 from 1922 to 1935. Imported from Belgium from the 1950s to 1974, today's SA-22s are made in Japan. Shown is the gorgeous Grade IV model.

MARLIN XT

From small-game to one-hole groups on paper, the bolt-action Marlin XT in .22-caliber gets the job done. The gun features a tubular magazine that'll hold 25 rounds of Short, 19 rounds of Long, or 17 rounds of LR. It also has a full pistol grip with palm swell and stippled gripping areas.

SAVAGE RASCAL

What a terrific gun to start young shooters with! Savage's new single-shot .22 LR bolt-action Rascal has a fore-end just made for small hands, as well as a short 31½-inch overall length and a light weight of 2.66 pounds.

CZ 512

When you're ready to graduate from .22 LR plinkers, then CZ's 512 is the next step up. Trim and lightweight, thanks to a light-weight, fiberglass-reinforced polymer lower and an alloy upper, this modernistic rifle is efficient on paper or small game and garnering strong reviews for accuracy from shooters every-where. A .22 WMR version is also available.

KIMBER MODEL 8400 SONORA

Sometimes you just can't get close enough. Or maybe distance is just your thing. Either way, the Model 8400 Sonora from Kimber was made for you, with a satin, fluted, stainless steel bull barrel and a match-grade chamber drilled for .25-06, 7mm Rem., or .300 Win. Mag.

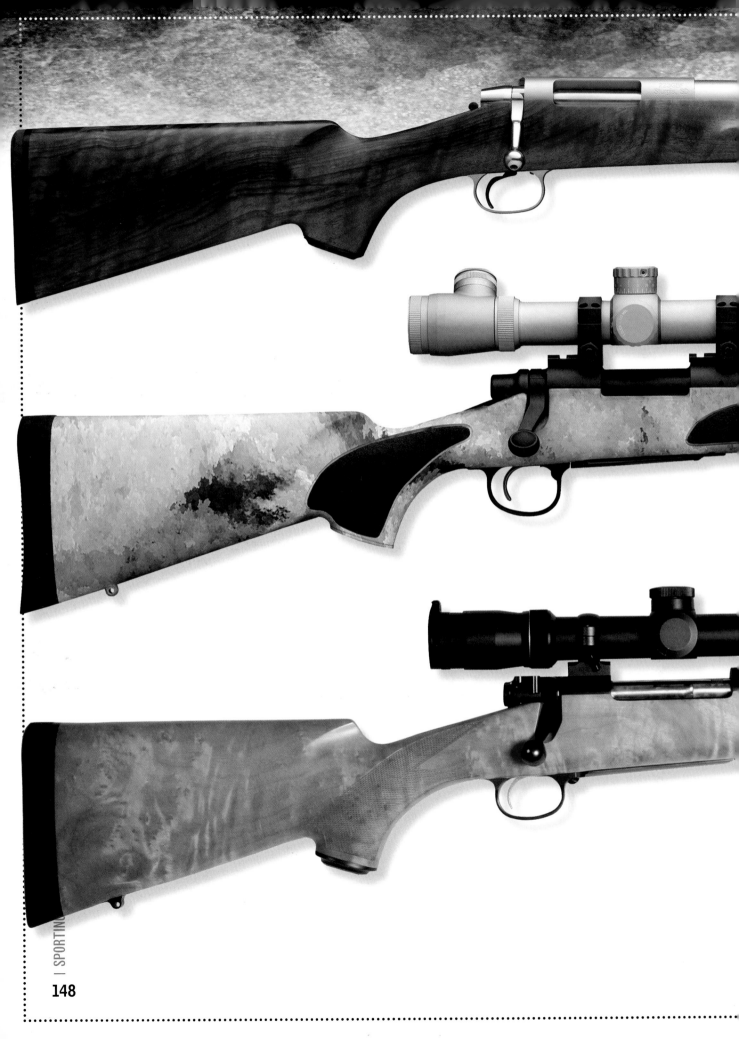

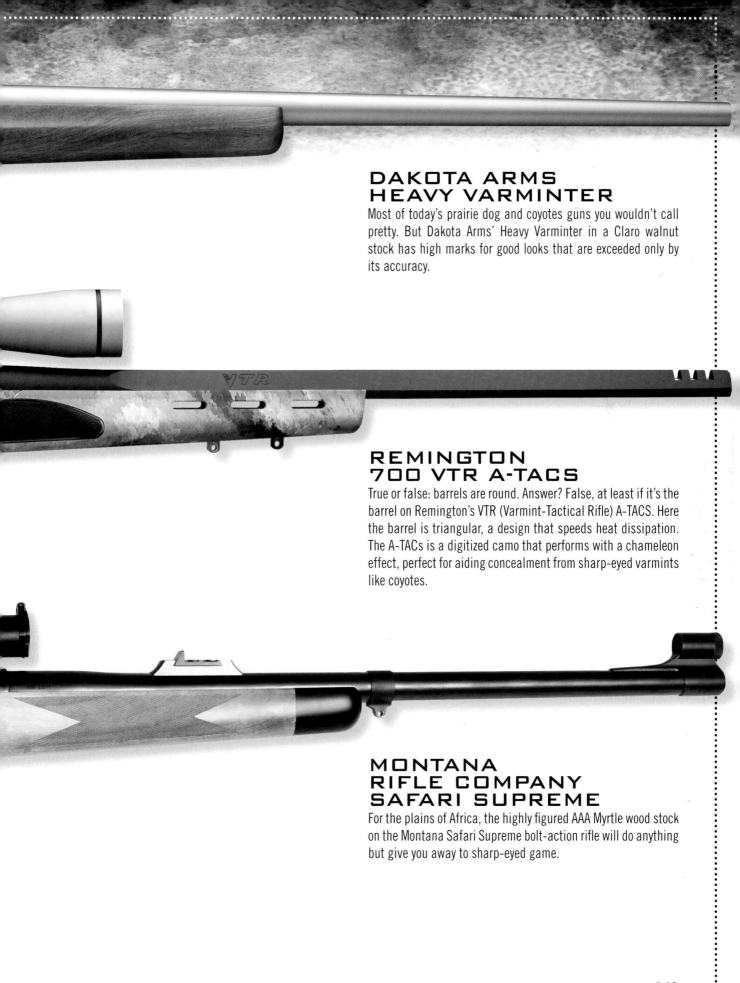

DAKOTA ARMS
HEAVY VARMINTER

Most of today's prairie dog and coyotes guns you wouldn't call pretty. But Dakota Arms' Heavy Varminter in a Claro walnut stock has high marks for good looks that are exceeded only by its accuracy.

REMINGTON
700 VTR A-TACS

True or false: barrels are round. Answer? False, at least if it's the barrel on Remington's VTR (Varmint-Tactical Rifle) A-TACS. Here the barrel is triangular, a design that speeds heat dissipation. The A-TACs is a digitized camo that performs with a chameleon effect, perfect for aiding concealment from sharp-eyed varmints like coyotes.

MONTANA
RIFLE COMPANY
SAFARI SUPREME

For the plains of Africa, the highly figured AAA Myrtle wood stock on the Montana Safari Supreme bolt-action rifle will do anything but give you away to sharp-eyed game.

MOSSBERG NIGHT TRAIN

The short-action Night Train from Mossberg comes with a factory mounted 4-16X50mm scope, attached bipod, and sling. Its magazine is top-loading for super quick reloads.

SAVAGE AXIS

A whittled fore-end, sculptured pistol grip, and skeletonized bolt shank all help reduce weight on the Savage Axis, which comes in at a scant 6½ pounds. There are lots of calibers to choose from, and the Axis now comes in a left-hand model.

SAVAGE 10/110 PREDATOR HUNTER

Gotta love the cartridge offerings in the Savage 10/110 Predator Hunter Max 1. This all-camo bolt in both right- and left-hand models comes in .204 Ruger, .22-250, .223, .243, .260 Rem., 6.5 Creedmoor, and 6.5x284 Norma. Varmints watch out!

BLASER R8

Blaser perfects the bolt operation with its decidedly luxurious R8 model. Designed to allow the shooter a relaxed posture and minimal hand movement from trigger to bolt when cycling, quick follow-up shots are an understatement. Like it's single-shot brethren Model K95, the R8 has swappable barrels and calibers, but several other features set this gun far, far apart from the vast crowd of bolt-action rifles out there. To begin with, the R8 features an integrated magazine/trigger assembly that drops cleanly out of the gun in one piece. This prevents unauthorized use and safe storage for transport, plus adds an extra measure of overall safety, as the gun cannot be cocked with the assembly out. Every magazine has a dust cover that slides over its cavity in the lower receiver when it's absent, and the magazines have a double lock that prevent accidental expulsion when in use. Add to that a desmodromic mechanical trigger mechanism that resets the trigger upon cycling without the use of a spring, which can be compromised by harsh temperatures and debris, and you have perhaps one of the most reliable, accurate, and user-friendly bolt-actions in the world.

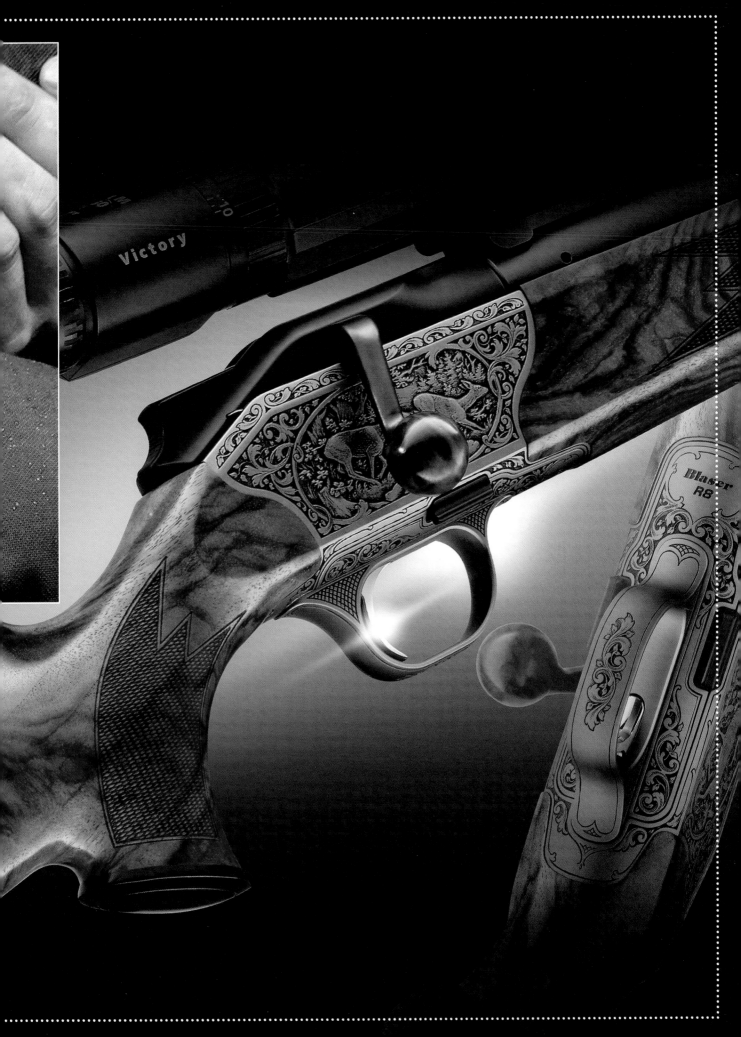

MONTANA
RIFLE COMPANY
RIDGELINE

Can you get accurate shots at distance out of a light-weight rifle? You can if it's a 6 pound 2 ounce Ridgeline from Montana Rifle Company. The makers employed an M1999 breaching system that controls the barrel whip inherent in light rifles.

MARLIN X7

Marlin is famous for its lever-actions, but its X7 Series has taken the bolt community by storm. Button rifling, fluted bolts, pillar bedding and adjustable triggers rank these rifles as best-in-class.

RUGER 77/357

Ruger's 77/357 bolt-action .357 Mag. rifle is a smart choice for medium-sized game in heavy cover, thanks to its stainless hardware and a flush-fit rotary magazine that won't get caught on clothing or brush.

BLASER R93 VARMINT

Long-range precision is what varmint hunting is all about. Blaser's high-speed straight-pull bolt-action R93 in a Varmint configuration options an adjustable stock, bipod, Mag-Na-Port ported and free-floated barrel, and wooden bolt knob, to name just a few custom upgrades.

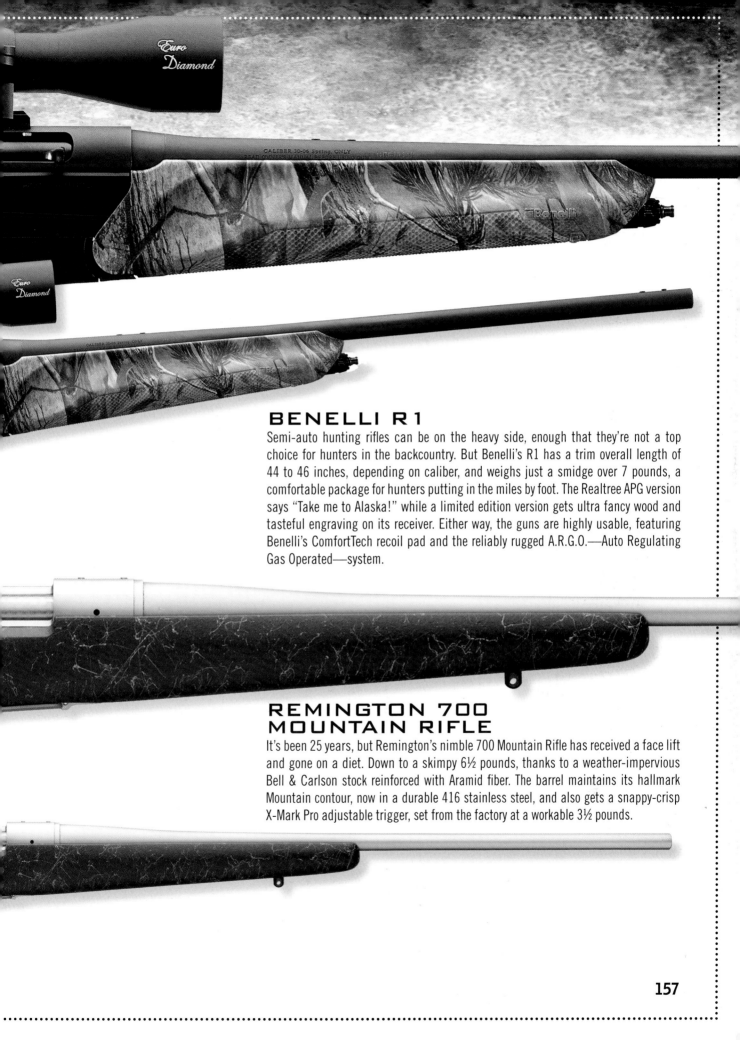

BENELLI R1

Semi-auto hunting rifles can be on the heavy side, enough that they're not a top choice for hunters in the backcountry. But Benelli's R1 has a trim overall length of 44 to 46 inches, depending on caliber, and weighs just a smidge over 7 pounds, a comfortable package for hunters putting in the miles by foot. The Realtree APG version says "Take me to Alaska!" while a limited edition version gets ultra fancy wood and tasteful engraving on its receiver. Either way, the guns are highly usable, featuring Benelli's ComfortTech recoil pad and the reliably rugged A.R.G.O.—Auto Regulating Gas Operated—system.

REMINGTON 700 MOUNTAIN RIFLE

It's been 25 years, but Remington's nimble 700 Mountain Rifle has received a face lift and gone on a diet. Down to a skimpy 6½ pounds, thanks to a weather-impervious Bell & Carlson stock reinforced with Aramid fiber. The barrel maintains its hallmark Mountain contour, now in a durable 416 stainless steel, and also gets a snappy-crisp X-Mark Pro adjustable trigger, set from the factory at a workable 3½ pounds.

REMINGTON MODEL 700 SPECIAL EDITIONS

Big Green Remington is almost giddy with anniversary celebrations these days. Its two newest include Model 700 celebrations.

First is the limited edition Model 700 BDL 50th Anniversary rifle in 7mm, and it's one you may never want to shoot, with well-figured "B" grade American walnut, period-correct fleur-de-lis checkering, white-line spacer at the butt-pad, and black fore-end and pistol grip caps. The 700 BDL, first in production in 1962, has sold in numbers exceeding five million, and its reputation for accuracy and longevity are nearly beyond reproach.

The second Model 700 cheers the anniversary of a cartridge, the now 100-year-old .375 Holland & Holland Magnum, a favorite cartridge of African hunters who loved its do-all capabilities. It was originally introduced by the British firm in both flanged and belted rimless configurations, the former for use in double rifles, the latter for magazined rifles like this Remington.

KIMBER MODEL 84L
CLASSIC SELECT

Kimber's 84L Classic Select grade is one to be handed down through the generations, thanks to its Grade A French walnut, hand-cut 20 lines-per-inch checkering, and a match-grade chamber and barrel. If you don't want to splurge for the extra nice wood, then Kimber's Model 84L Classic is the right choice. If you like to hike while you hunt, this one comes in at a scant 6 pounds 2 ounces. It's available in two cartridges every bit as classic as the rifle itself, the .270 and .30-06.

BERETTA 1873
RENEGADE LEVER RIFLE

It's "Spaghetti Western" fun all day long with Beretta's 1873 Renegade Short Rifle. Made especially for SASS matches, the gun's quick and short lever throw is a welcome partner to any cowboy action shooter's arsenal, especially with the traditional looks of the case-colored receiver. The original gun was chambered in the fairly powerful blackpowder metallic cartridge .44-40, its success ensured not only by this rifle, at the time, but also the likewise introduction, by Colt's, of a six-chambered revolver in the same round. This modern version is over-the-counter friendly, though, with model available in .45 LC or .357 Magnum.

BERETTA 1866 LEVER RIFLE

Claimed to be the first rifle to bear the Winchester name, the Model 1866 became best-known by the moniker "Yellowboy." Uberti makes reproductions today, marketed under its own name and others, such as Beretta, and it can be found in both rifle and carbine lengths. The gun gained fame, not only for its unique, high-polished brass frame, but for a new type of loading gate designed by Nelson King, who was a Winchester plant supervisor of the era. This gun is considered to be the very first cowboy gun, seeing lively duty in saddle scabbards across the nineteenth-century American frontier.

THOMPSON/CENTER ICON WARLORD

Accuracy nuts will go, well, nuts for Thompson/Center's Icon Warlord. The gun boasts a cement-like foundation for accuracy, with an aluminum bedding block in its flat-bottomed stock locking into the receiver's recoil lugs. Half-inch MOA at 100 yards was certified with each gun.

SAKO FINLIGHT

Sako's Finlight ST gets spot-on accuracy from a unique recoil lug and a flat-bottomed, stainless receiver mated precisely to the synthetic stock. A palm swell and grip panels help, too, when a record book sheep is 400 yards over on the next mountain. There's an admirable range of cartridges available, a little bit of everything from prairie dog appropriate .22-250 on up to Africa's favorite, the .375 H&H.

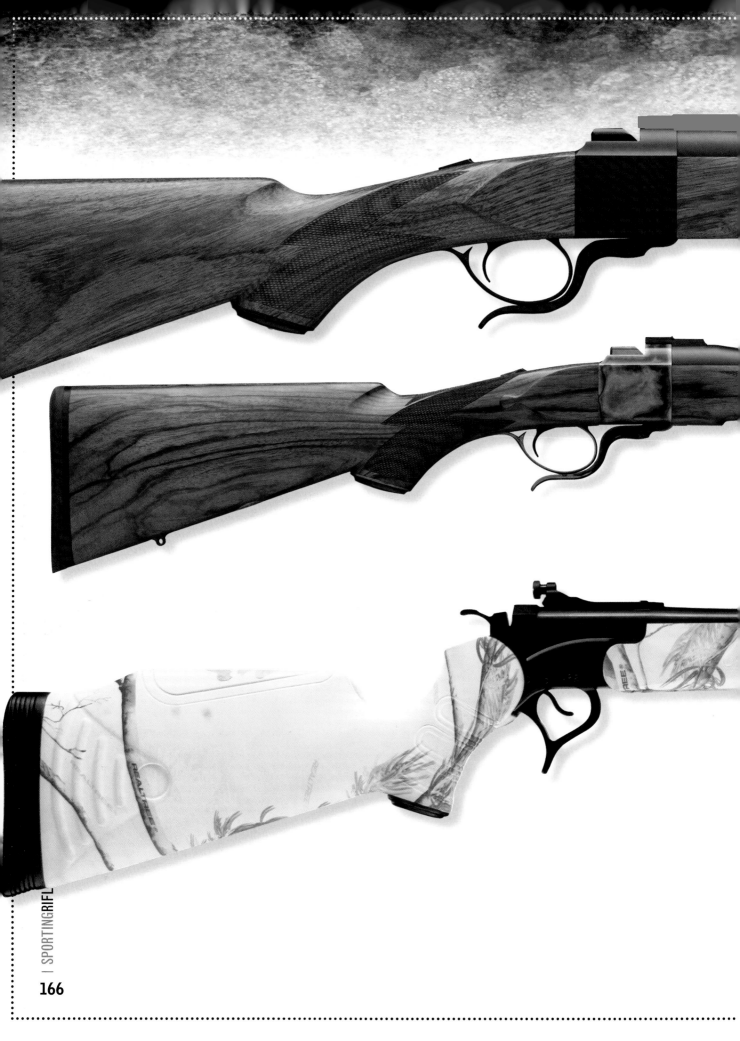

DAKOTA ARMS MODEL 10

Dakota Arms' falling block, Mannlicher stocked, single-shot Model 10 is an ideal gun for those who foot hunt over the distances. In calibers .17 HMR to .404 Dakota, there's no game this gun can't handle. If your traveling and hunting needs benefit from compact transport, then Dakota Arm's provides convenience, superb quality, and the caliber flexibility in its take-down Model 76 Traveler.

THOMPSON/CENTER HOT SHOT

Dads who want to get their daughters interested in shooting would be wise to pick the .22 LR Hotshot from Thompson/Center. Not only will you get an accurate and safe gun for first introductions, but what girl can refuse pink camo these days?!

MAGNUM RESEARCH MAGNUMLITE

Magnum Research's MagnumLite .22 LR rifle is definitely a head-turner. And if looks weren't enough, this rifle has a graphite barrel—that's right, graphite—with claims of super accuracy and faster cooling over steel barrels.

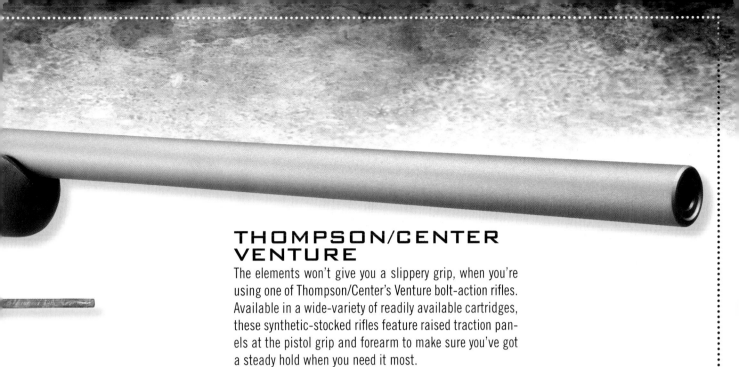

THOMPSON/CENTER VENTURE

The elements won't give you a slippery grip, when you're using one of Thompson/Center's Venture bolt-action rifles. Available in a wide-variety of readily available cartridges, these synthetic-stocked rifles feature raised traction panels at the pistol grip and forearm to make sure you've got a steady hold when you need it most.

TIKKA T3 HUNTER

Tikka's T3 Hunter is simply beautiful, with a high-gloss blued barrel, burled wood, and ergonomic checkering at the hand points. It also has a free-floating match-grade barrel and adjustable trigger to make every shot count.

WINCHESTER MODEL 1885

Part Old West buffalo hunter, part new world blackpowder cartridge metallic silhouette competitor, Winchester's case colored 1885 in the Traditional Sporter version (above) comes in .45-70 Gov't., .38-55 Win., .45-90 BPCR, and .40-65 Win. It wears a full round barrel at 28 inches in length and a Marble's gold bead front sight. For the serious competitor knocking over steel rams at distance, the Black Powder Cartridge Rifle (directly below) gets a half round/half octagon 30-inch barrel, a spirit level front sight, and a Soule windage style Creedmoor rear sight that's designed for 1/4 MOA windage and 1/2 MOA elevation adjustments.

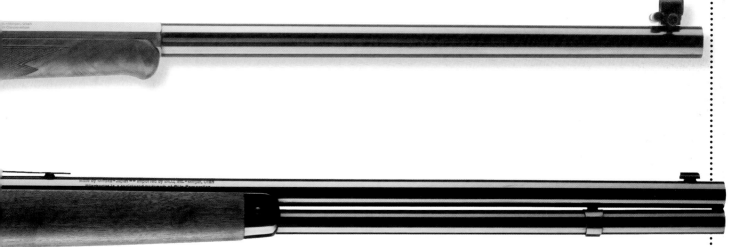

WINCHESTER MODEL 1886 SHORT RIFLE

More than authentic, the 1886 Short Rifle is a top choice in lever-actions for cowboy action competitors. The 20-inch barrel is trim and maneuverable, great for fast-action courses of fire, and the crescent butt-plate hugs the shooter's shoulder pocket for a firm mount and sure aim.

MONTANA RIFLE COMPANY
XWR XTREME WEATHER RIFLE

Bad weather and dangerous game are like two peas in a pod. Take them both on in style with the Xtreme Weather Rifle (XWR) from custom maker Montana Rifle Company. These dead-on rifles feature Belle and Carlson carbon fiber stocks with a full-length aluminum bedding block.

MARLIN 1895

Horseback hunts provide lots of advantages, not the least of which is your horse's ability to carry more gear than you can. One item to add to your pack list is the Marlin 1895 SBL stainless and laminate lever rifle in the bear-stopping .45-70 Gov't. round. A long Picatinny rail lends plenty of variety to scope mounts and eye relief distances. A similar version is Marlin's true-to-history 1895 Cowboy lever whose nine-round magazine also lines up the .45-70 Gov't. round. This straight-grip model gets decked out with a Marble semi-buckhorn rear and Marble carbine front sight, but if you're aging and need a scope, the gun comes drilled and tapped, too.

MONTANA RIFLE COMPANY SAFARI SUPREME TAKE-DOWN

Montana Rifle Company founder Keith Sipes self-designed controlled-round feed Montana Action is strong as can be. Give it a whirl in the take-down Safari Supreme next time Cape Buffalo are slated to be a problem for you.

MONTANA RIFLE COMPANY AMERICAN STANDARD & WOODLAND

When you can't find what you're looking for, you make it yourself. Or at least that's what Montana Rifle Company founder Keith Sipes did when he couldn't find the Mauser '98 actions he liked to work with. Today, his own action can be found in the American Standard rifle, with black walnut stock and 22 cartridge variations. Want more bang for your bucks? Put a glass-bedded custom action in a AAA walnut stock with beautiful fleur-de-lis checkering in the Woodland version.

WINCHESTER MODEL 70 SAFARI EXPRESS

When Africa's dangerous game is on the menu, the gun you choose needs to be up to the task. Winchester's Model 70 Safari Express has all the reliability you'd expect in this revered action, but at nine pounds, this version is better able to help with the recoil of the .416 Rigby, .458 Win. Mag., or .375 H&H it chambers.

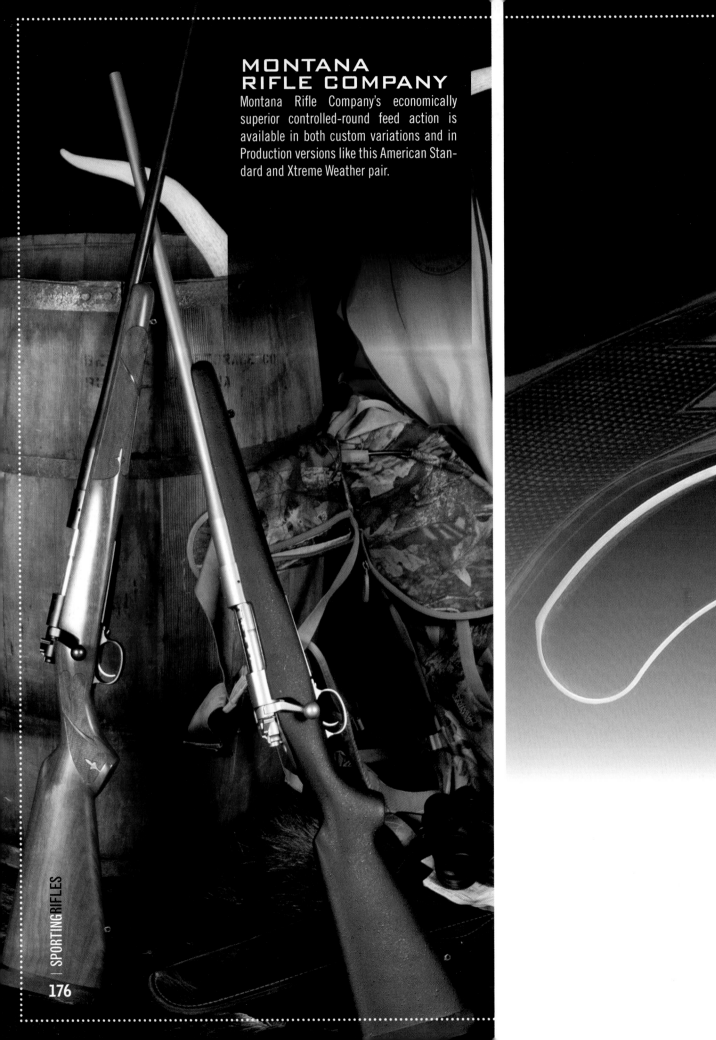

MONTANA
RIFLE COMPANY

Montana Rifle Company's economically superior controlled-round feed action is available in both custom variations and in Production versions like this American Standard and Xtreme Weather pair.

BROWNING BLR WHITE GOLD MEDALLION

The Browning BLR lever rifle is not only a super choice for close-quarters hunting, thanks to its trim 6½ pounds and short 20- or 22-inch barrels (depending on caliber), it's also an heirloom in the making in the engraved White Gold Medallion version.

MERKEL K3

Merkel's single-shots are a walking hunter's dream. These diminutive, single-shot rifles, available in a half-stock or Mannlicher stock design, are lightweight, beautifully crafted, and highly accurate. They are a premium option for the world-traveling hunter.

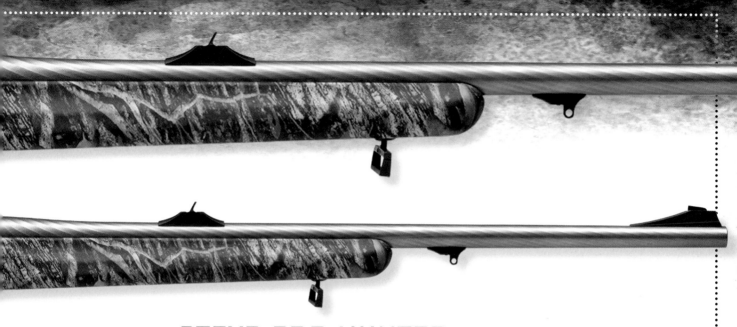

STEYR PRO HUNTER

This Pro Hunter is the "working-class" line of guns from premium maker Steyr. In dozens of configurations, from the Varmint to the Big-Bore to the ultra-portable Scout (with its integral bipod) and the super tough Pro African and Alaskan models in the hard-hitting .338 RCM and .375 Ruger rounds can tackle any creature with teeth, claws, or horns, any weather from sandstorm to snow storm, and any amount of other abuse you can think of to dish out to it. Combined with unique styling and pin-point accuracy, these special rifles are a notch or three above the usual crowd.

ANSCHÜTZ 1780

Anschütz is, without doubt, a brand known worldwide for its competition winning accuracy. But not only does the company make the guns that take home gold medals, it applies its genius to guns for hunting, as well. Take, for instance, the drop-dead gorgeous thumb-hole stocked model 1780. Available in .308, .30-06, 8x57IS, and 9.3x62, the stock design is intended to optimally position the shooter's hand for superb trigger control, in the same manner every time you put your hand on the rifle. The design also features support for the middle finger of the trigger hand, adding much stability to this platform. Now, if only you could stop drooling over the fiddlebacked lines in the wood and take the time to shoot it ... .

WEATHERBY MARK V

It's been more than 50 years, but Roy Weatherby's famous Mark V has come home again to California. Manufactured in Minnesota since 1999, with production in Germany, Japan, and other U.S. locations since Roy first introduced the gun out of his original production facilities in South Gate, California, in 1958, Roy's son, Ed, made the decision to bring this wonderful sporting rifle back to its Sunshine State roots. Weatherby began production of the Mark V action, known around the globe as the strongest bolt action ever made, in the firm's Paso Robles facility, in October 2011. Welcome home, Mark V!

ESSAY TEXT BY TOM TURPIN

CUSTOM & ENGRAVED GUNS

Tom Turpin has a Midas touch, at least when it comes to having access to some of the finest custom guns this world has ever seen. True, most of us will probably never own one of these firearms, but that shouldn't stop anyone from admiring the craftsmanship and artwork that goes into these extraordinary firearms. After all, most of us will never own a Ferrari, but it doesn't mean you can't love looking at one and dreaming a little.

We here at *Gun Digest* books are forever thankful that Tom contributes a most outstanding photographic essay on custom guns each year to the *Gun Digest* annual edition. It is one of the favorite entries of that book's loyal following, and, so, we thought nothing would be more appropriate than to gather up and include a compilation of Tom's past work here in the *Gun Digest Illustrated Guide to Modern Firearms*.
—*Jennifer L.S. Pearsall, Editor, Gun Digest Books*

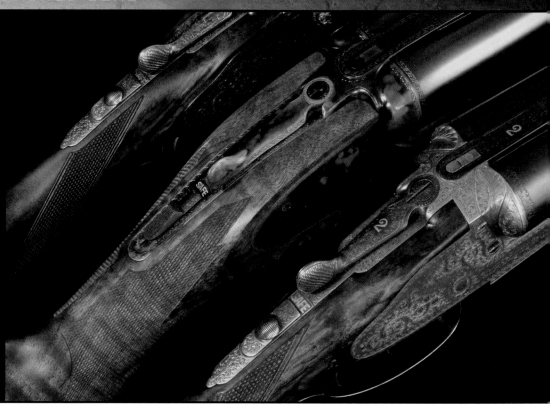

(right) This photo shows the new U.S.A.-made Searcy "rising bite" double flanked on either side by an original Rigby double shotgun featuring the rising bite they offered to the market at the turn of the twentieth century. This pair of original Rigby doubles was made in 1903. The Searcy was finished in 2010.

(opposite) A close-up photo of the Searcy-produced Rigby Bissell "rising bite" locking system. Due to the complexity and difficulty of manufacture, to my knowledge, none have been made in more than a half-century, probably closer to 75 years or so.

PHOTOS BY STEVE HELSLEY.

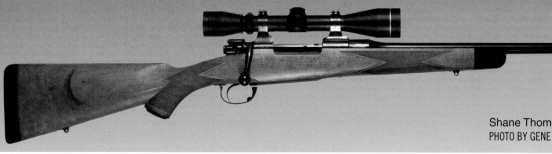

Shane Thompson FN 98 Mauser.
PHOTO BY GENE WRIGHT.

Shane Thompson

Shane Thompson is a very talented young gunmaker. He does both stock and metal-work and he does each with equal meticulousness. The rifle shown here is a good example of his work in both materials. He started with a very early FN Model 98 Mauser action that he blueprinted, truing all the surfaces. He recontoured and reshaped a 1909 Argentine set of bottom metal and fitted it to the action. He fabricated scope rings and bases from bar stock in his shop and fitted them to the action. He chambered the barrel for the .270 Winchester cartridge, fitted a three-position safety, and finally hand polished the action and barrel.

The stock on this rifle is a bit unusual. It is fabricated from a piece of mesquite that grew on the client's ranch. The client cut and sealed the wood many years ago and insisted on using it for the stock. Shane whittled out the stock and fitted it with a genuine horn fore-end tip and grip cap. He checkered it in a point pattern 24 and added a mullered border. He finished his work by mounting a Leupold 3-9x variable power scope. The finished rifle weighs 7 pounds 11 ounces without the scope, and eight pounds 10 ounces with it. The astute viewer might note that the rifle is a right hand action, but stocked for a southpaw. That's the way the client learned to shoot and the way he wanted it done. Finally, Gary Griffiths engraved the rifle.

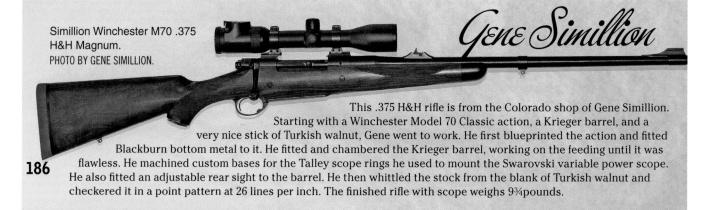

Simillion Winchester M70 .375 H&H Magnum.
PHOTO BY GENE SIMILLION.

Gene Simillion

This .375 H&H rifle is from the Colorado shop of Gene Simillion. Starting with a Winchester Model 70 Classic action, a Krieger barrel, and a very nice stick of Turkish walnut, Gene went to work. He first blueprinted the action and fitted Blackburn bottom metal to it. He fitted and chambered the Krieger barrel, working on the feeding until it was flawless. He machined custom bases for the Talley scope rings he used to mount the Swarovski variable power scope. He also fitted an adjustable rear sight to the barrel. He then whittled the stock from the blank of Turkish walnut and checkered it in a point pattern at 26 lines per inch. The finished rifle with scope weighs 9¾ pounds.

Butch Searcy

The rifle shown here is a bit of a departure from those normally found in custom side-by-side rifles. Although it can be and usually is a "bespoke" gun, and therefore made for a specific client, this one is the first modern-made double rifle that has appeared in the custom gun section under my byline that I can recall. Butch Searcy has been making double rifles for a number of years. Over time, his rifles have developed a reputation as solid, affordable, working double rifles.

This rifle, though, is the first of a new breed of Searcy doubles, and for two reasons: it is a sidelock gun instead of the more often encountered boxlock (and even though Butch has produced sidelock guns before from time to time). What really sets this one apart, and something that no one has produced in at least a half-century or more, not even the Brits, is that this rifle features a Rigby-Bissell patent (1879) rising bite third-bite. It is my understanding that the "new" London Rigby firm is producing a Rigby double featuring this locking system, as well. I've seen photos of it in the works, but don't know if it is finished as yet. At any rate this Searcy rifle is complete and chambered for the .470 Nitro Express cartridge.

PHOTO BY MUSTAFA BILAL, TURK'S HEAD PRODUCTIONS.

Trez Hensley/
Ed LaPour Colt Lightning.

Hensley

...ustom stockmakers over the last couple decades has
...ley. His stocks have been on many of our very best
...win has been stricken with Parkinson's disease and can
...his fabulous custom stocks. However, the family name
...e custom gun trade is in good hands, as his son Trez has
...arwin had to leave off.

...custom rifle began as an original Colt Lightning cham-
...CF cartridge and made in 1878. The metalwork is mostly
...en cleaned up a bit by both Trez and by Ed LaPour.
...ed the wonderful engraving and gold inlay work on the
...crafted the extraordinary stock from a really nice piece
...He checkered the stock in a point pattern at 26 lines per
...ed border. The shadow-line cheekpiece is very unusual
... double radius, rather than the usual single. Trez is well
...on the tradition of excellence established by his father.

Hans Doesel

Hans Doesel is a relatively young German engraver who studied under my old friend Erich Boessler. I believe that he apprenticed under Erich, as well as studied for his Master certificate under him. He's been a Master engraver for several years now and is turning out some fastidious work. He is very versatile and can do traditional Germanic sculpting in deep relief, as well as delicate bulino work. Shown here are two examples of his artistry.

(top) A Doesel Sauer Model 202 action featuring rather typical Germanic gold line inlay work in combination with the much less common bulino game scenes. Framing both is profuse scrollwork. All the work is beautifully done.

(bottom) A Doesel Floorplate from a Model 70 Winchester that is mostly bulino work depicting an African scene that features three Cape buffalo. Included is moderate gold line inlay and larger scroll decoration, including a fleur de lis motif.

PHOTOS BY HANS DOESEL.

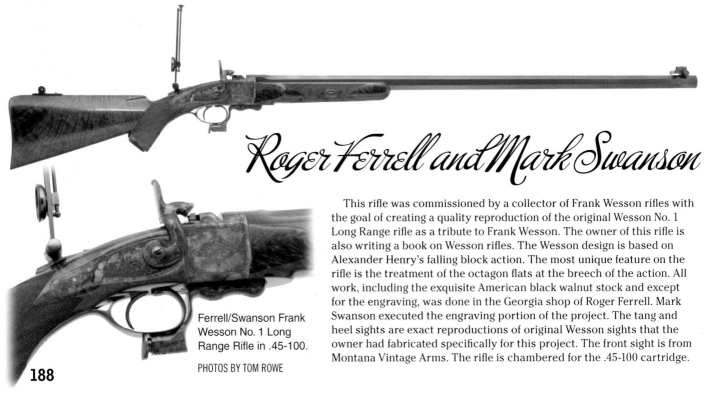

Roger Ferrell and Mark Swanson

This rifle was commissioned by a collector of Frank Wesson rifles with the goal of creating a quality reproduction of the original Wesson No. 1 Long Range rifle as a tribute to Frank Wesson. The owner of this rifle is also writing a book on Wesson rifles. The Wesson design is based on Alexander Henry's falling block action. The most unique feature on the rifle is the treatment of the octagon flats at the breech of the action. All work, including the exquisite American black walnut stock and except for the engraving, was done in the Georgia shop of Roger Ferrell. Mark Swanson executed the engraving portion of the project. The tang and heel sights are exact reproductions of original Wesson sights that the owner had fabricated specifically for this project. The front sight is from Montana Vintage Arms. The rifle is chambered for the .45-100 cartridge.

Ferrell/Swanson Frank Wesson No. 1 Long Range Rifle in .45-100.

PHOTOS BY TOM ROWE

Barry Lee Hands

Shown here are two examples of the artistry of Montana engraver Barry Lee Hands. Considering that he's about the same age as my son, it's remarkable that he has progressed so much in such a short time. A very versatile engraver, he can do most any style of engraving, and do it very well indeed.

This little Colt .25 auto is a perfect canvas for Barry's exquisite floral and gold pattern, on both steel and pearl. This work is as good as it gets.
PHOTO BY BARRY LEE HANDS.

It is probably unfair to show just the buttplate engraving on this rifle. The scene depicts the annual collection of winter's meat by the plains Indians, acquired by driving buffalo off a cliff. This scene is done in high relief and is immaculate.
PHOTO BY BARRY LEE HANDS.

Terry Wieland and James Flynn

PHOTO BY TERRY WIELAND.

This rifle is the brainchild of outdoors writer Terry Wieland. Terry is a Canadian by birth and an avid Anglophile. In addition to being a fantastic writer, he is also a history buff and delights in doing themed projects. This rifle is such a project and is called his "Beau Brummell" rifle. Brummell, for those unaware, was the arbiter of English men's fashion in the late 18th century and into the early 19th century. His motto was "if people turn to look at you on the street, you are not well dressed." He left behind an England where men dressed in austere but superbly cut clothing, a style still followed there today.

Wieland/Flynn
"Beau Brummel Rifle"
on FN Supreme Mauser action.

Wieland, in collaboration with Louisiana gunmaker James Flynn, transferred Brummell's concept in clothing to the making of this rifle. Their object was to demonstrate the time, effort, and skill that go into making a custom rifle both functional and aesthetic perfection, like a Beau Brummell dinner jacket. Starting with an FN Supreme Mauser action, a Danny Pedersen .25-caliber cut-rifled barrel, they had Bill Dowtin of Old World Walnut personally select the blank of walnut for the project. James Flynn then fashioned all the components into a functional masterpiece that would fully fit Beau Brummell's sense of styling. I like to call it quiet elegance.

Reto Buehler

Reto Buehler began this project with a Granite Mountain Arms Magnum Mauser action, a custom contoured Pac Nor barrel, and a fabulous stick of Turkish walnut. He first extended the tangs to the action and to the bottom metal. He also machined the quarter rib from bar stock. The GMA action was worked over to feed the big .500 Jeffery cartridges like a hot knife through butter. He then fashioned the terrific stock in the English styling. He checkered the stock in a 20 lines per inch flat topped design. Reto finished the job by rust bluing the metalwork and nitre bluing the ejector and extractor spring. It just doesn't get any better than this.

Reto Buehler .500 Jeffery on GMA action.
PHOTO BY MUSTAFA BILAL, TURKS HEAD PRODUCTIONS.

Mike Dubber

Mike Dubber, from Indiana, is a super-talented engraver. Over the past several years that I've known him, he has matured from a really good engraver into a really great one, and much more quickly than most I have known. This photo is a recent example of his exemplary work. He started with a 2nd Generation Colt SAA and a theme of the Lakota Sioux last buffalo hunt. He even had a pencil drawing of the last Sioux buffalo hunter, drawn by an unknown artist in the 1800s. The 5½-inch barreled revolver has been heavily inlaid with gold and platinum and fitted with custom sambar stag grips. It is chambered for the .45 Colt cartridge and is finished in French Gray.

Mike Dubber 2nd Gen SAA in .45 Colt.
PHOTO BY TOM ALEXANDER.

Gary Goudy M70
Featherweight in .30-06.

Gary Goudy

Above is a lovely custom rifle from the shop of stockmaker Gary Goudy. The rifle was a Model 70 Featherweight .30-06, and the barrel was so accurate that it was retained. Gary fitted an ancient set of Ted Blackburn bottom metal to the action. Note that it does not use a straddle floorplate, something that Ted hasn't produced in years. The stock is checkered in a very nice point pattern with mullered borders. Bob Evans engraved the rifle.

As for the lever gun to the right, this is most likely the most unusual custom rifle that you'll ever come across. Gary Goudy's client wanted a custom BB gun for his grandson. Gary came up with a brand new Daisy Red Ryder BB gun and stocked it with a magnificent piece of Turkish walnut. I've been around the horn a time or two, but this is the only custom BB gun I've ever come across.

PHOTOS BY GARY BOLSTER.

Goudy Daisy Red Ryder.

Paul Lindke

Stockmaker Paul Lindke started this project with a pre-'64 Model 70 barreled action chambered for the .270 Winchester cartridge. The factory barrel was so accurate that it was retained. He picked up a very nice stick of California English walnut from Steve Heilmann and added a McFarland steel skeleton buttplate, a Leupold VXIII 2.5-8x scope, and Leupold double dovetail mounts. He stocked the rifle, adding an ebony fore-end tip, and checkered the stock in a 24 lines per inch fleur de lis pattern with ribbons.

Lindke pre-'64 M70 in .270 Winchester.
PHOTO BY TOM ALEXANDER.

191

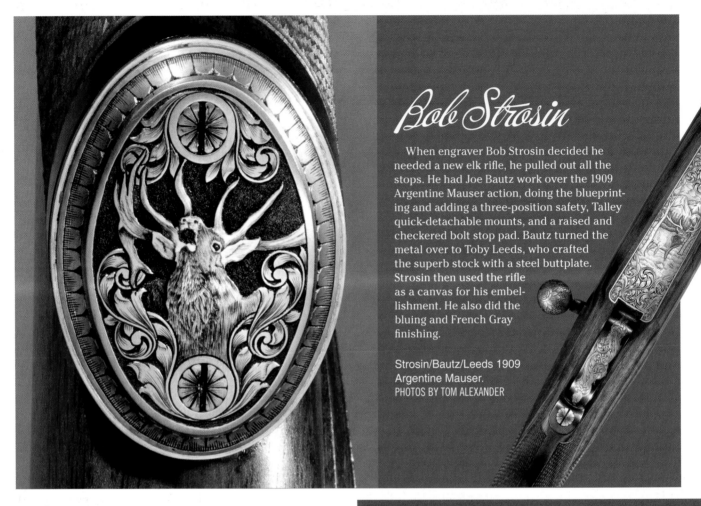

Bob Strosin

When engraver Bob Strosin decided he needed a new elk rifle, he pulled out all the stops. He had Joe Bautz work over the 1909 Argentine Mauser action, doing the blueprinting and adding a three-position safety, Talley quick-detachable mounts, and a raised and checkered bolt stop pad. Bautz turned the metal over to Toby Leeds, who crafted the superb stock with a steel buttplate. Strosin then used the rifle as a canvas for his embellishment. He also did the bluing and French Gray finishing.

Strosin/Bautz/Leeds 1909 Argentine Mauser.
PHOTOS BY TOM ALEXANDER

Lee Griffiths

Lee Griffiths is a very talented and versatile engraver. Shown here are two examples that emphasize the wide range of engraving styles that he is more than capable of executing to perfection. The first photo is of an L.C. Smith double 12-gauge shotgun, which Griffiths engraved in traditional scrollwork, bulino scenes, and gold line inlay work. There is also heavy chiseled sculpting on the fences and the breaking lever. The second example, a Perazzi over/under, features much more contemporary engraving, combining traditional scrollwork with a heavily sculpted trigger guard bow and multi-metal inlay work, including those of gold, platinum, silver, and copper. Both pieces are exquisitely done.

(above) Lee Griffiths L.C. Smith 12-gauge.

(left) Griffiths Perazzi over/under.

PHOTOS COURTESY OF LEE GRIFFITHS

David Norin

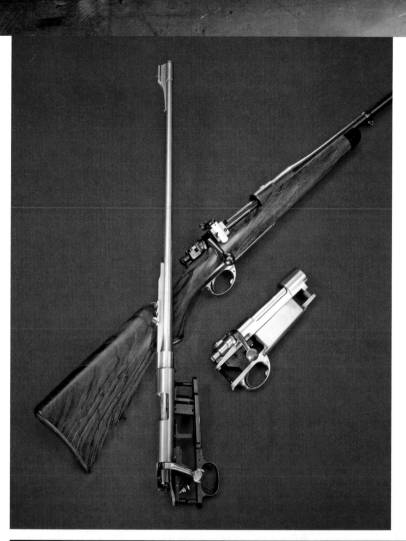

Chicago-area gunmaker David Norin can and does do everything on a custom gun except the engraving. Shown here are some examples of his work. The action is a Standard Model, which came out of the great Oberndorf Werke, in the 1930s. Norin fitted a Fisher round-bottom magazine and trigger guard assembly, added a new bolt knob suitably checkered, and polished, ground, and stoned the action to the stage shown in the photo. The barreled action is a Dakota .22 RF to which has been added a sculpted bolt knob, a quarter-rib with express sights, and added stoning and polishing. This barreled action will be stocked as a mini-African stalking rifle.

The completed rifle is a Mauser action 7x57, fitted with a Fisher round-bottom magazine and trigger guard assembly, an Oberndorf-style bolt knob, three-position safety, Blackburn trigger, and a Lyman 48 peep sight. The rifle is stocked in a very nice stick of Turkish walnut and checkered in a point pattern at 22 lines per inch. The rifle is intended to be a deep-woods deer rifle.

PHOTO BY TOM ALEXANDER

Al Lofgren

Al Lofgren is a superb stockmaker and long-time member of the American Custom Gunmakers Guild (ACGG). Al delights in crafting fine custom stocks in the Germanic style. He has crafted many stocks using the reinforcing side panels, very reminiscent of Mauser factory stocks from the early twentieth century. In preparing for this job and looking through Michael Petrov's fine book, *Custom Gunmakers of the 20th Century*, he came across an example of a Sauer-made rifle with metal sideplates inletted into the reinforcing panels of the stock and so decided to incorporate metal sideplates into this stock job, using a nice stick of walnut from Paul and Sharon Dressel. Steve Nelson did much of the metalwork, including the square-bridging work on the rear bridge. He also did the quarter-rib and installed the three-position safety, Talley scope mounts, and the Weaver 3x scope.

Lofgren Mauser with metal sideplates.
PHOTOS BY TOM ALEXANDER

Glenn Fewless

The rifle shown here is a very early Gibbs 1870 Farquharson, serial number 92. It is a well-traveled rifle. It went from England, where it was manufactured, to India, and from there to New Zealand, and from Kiwi-land to the U.S.A. The rifle is chambered for the .500 3-inch Black Powder Express. It was not in the best of condition when it arrived at the Wisconsin bench of metalsmith Glenn Fewless. He completely rebuilt the rifle, including fitting a 26-inch full-ribbed barrel. When Glenn finished the metalwork, he shipped the rifle to Illinois stockmaker Doug Mann. Doug crafted the magnificent stock from a superb stick of Turkish exhibition grade walnut. Working from the blank, he whittled out the stock keeping in mind the original Gibbs styling for the stock. He added the leather covered pad, ebony forend tip, and checkered the finished stock in a 24 LPI point pattern. The rifle as shown is still in the white, awaiting finishing instructions from the client.

Glenn Fewless Gibbs Farquharson in .500 BPE, still in the white.
PHOTO BY TOM ALEXANDER

Joe Rundell

Joe Rundell is a multi-talented guy. He crafts wonderful custom stocks, does superb metalsmithing, but above all, he is a master engraver. While I don't normally run photos of anything other than custom guns here, I liked this custom knife so well that I thought it would be permissible. Knives and guns go together like biscuits and gravy anyway. Scott Sawby, using Damascus steel forged by Devin Thomas, crafted this custom Damascus folder. The client for this knife wanted nudes on the scales and selected Joe Rundell to do the execution. He did a masterful job.

PHOTO BY TOM ALEXANDER

Roger Sampson began studying engraving under the watchful eye of Emma Achleithner, who had been trained in Ferlach, Austria. Roger became a member of the Firearms Engravers Guild of America (FEGA), in 1985, and has been a professional member since 1989. He currently serves on the board of FEGA. Although Roger has specialized for years in adorning miniature firearms, the one shown here is a full-size, original Winchester Model 1885, built in 1888. The rifle was built by Jim Westberg and checkered by Don Klein. Roger than engraved the rifle in a lovely scroll pattern. The rifle is currently in the white, awaiting a decision from the client on the final finish option.

Roger Sampson original Winchester Model 1885, still in the white.
PHOTO BY TOM ALEXANDER

Roger Sampson

Bob Evans Bob Evans has been a successful engraver for many years now. He is a long-time member of the Firearms Engravers Guild of America and has served as that Guild's Historian for many years.

This floorplate is typical of Bob Evans artistry. The rifle was custom crafted for a client by Gary Goudy on a Model 70 action. It is chambered for the ever-popular .30-06 cartridge and the client specified it was to be his deer rifle. Following that theme, Evans designed the pattern executed on the floorplate that features an engraved and gold inlaid buck head as the centerpiece. He complemented the deer scene with lovely scrollwork and gold line inlay.
PHOTO BY GARY BOLSTER.

A lovely matched set of Browning Citori over/under shotguns custom stocked for the client by Al Lind. They are a matched set, rather than a matched pair, as one gun is a 12-bore, and the other a 20-bore. The client provided the beautiful wood, two sticks of Iranian-grown thin-shelled walnut. Al told me that the biggest challenge was doing the skeleton butt-plates on these through-bolt stoked guns. The matching skeleton grip caps were not nearly as difficult.

PHOTOS BY TOM ALEXANDER

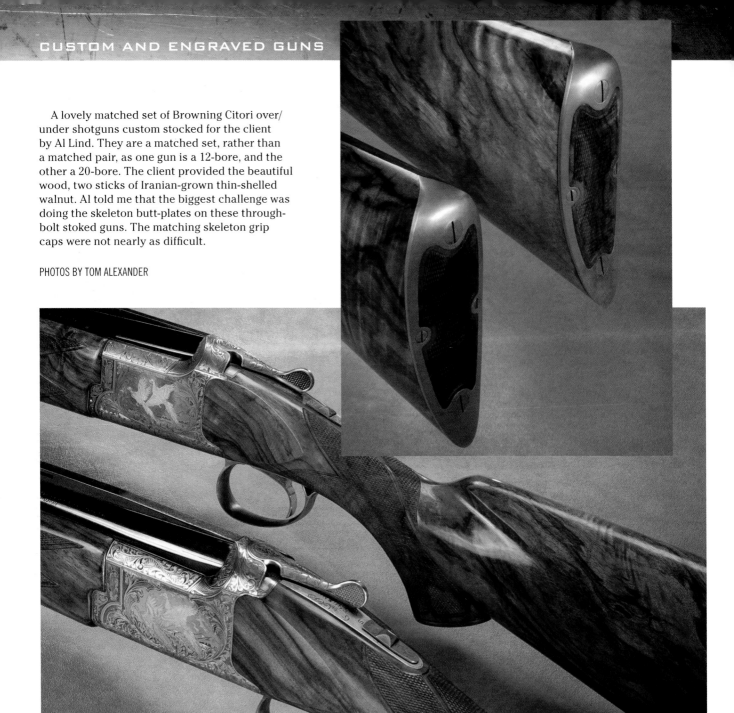

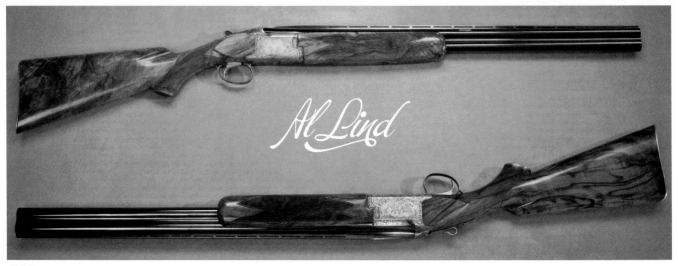

Each year, members of the American Custom Gunmakers Guild (ACGG) and the Firearms Engravers Guild of America (FEGA) build a special firearm that serves as the raffle rifle for the year. The team chosen to craft the project for a given year begins several years prior to the year it is offered as the raffle prize. This exquisite double rifle is No. 26 in the series and was presented to the holder of the winning raffle ticket in June 2011. Each ticket costs $20, and a maximum of 4,000 tickets will be sold.

For this project, Tony Fleming, Glenn Morovits, and Larry Peters comprised the project team. They decided to craft a working .470 Nitro Express double rifle that would be right at home on an African safari. The metal components were procured from Butch Searcy, raw from the factory. Metalsmith Tony Fleming converted this raw metal into a fine action, modeled after an early twentieth century boxlock express rifle. Peters regulated the twin barrels, and the gun delivers 2¾-inch groups at 100 yards—superb accuracy for a double rifle. Stockmaker Glenn Morovits crafted the stock from a super stick of Turkish walnut, chosen for its dark color and tight, dense grain. Finally, Larry Peters added the exquisite English-style scroll engraving in keeping with the tradition of double rifles. Gold inlay was added only at the safety. He modeled the engraving after a Joseph Lang & Son .577 BPE rifle, a gift to an Indian Prince, in 1898.

PHOTOS BY TOM ALEXANDER

Glenn Morovits • Larry Peters • Tony Fleming

This .264 Winchester Magnum rifle features the only Monte Carlo styled stock that gunmaker D'Arcy Echols has ever built. All the other stocks that he has crafted have been straight combed and purely classic in design. The client for this rifle is rather small in stature, and the Monte Carlo comb was necessary for him to properly use the scope. The rifle features a Model 70 action, Krieger barrel, Echols custom mounts and scope rings, and one of the last sets of bottom metal that Tom Burgess turned out before he passed. All other work on this rifle was accomplished in the Echols shop.

PHOTO COURTESY OF D'ARCY ECHOLS

D'Arcy Echols crafted this fine rifle in 1987. He started with a Sako L-79 action that was made for Browning Safari rifles. As such, it does not have the normal Sako dovetail scope mounting system on the bridges of the action. Echols fitted a Steve Wikert barrel (Fred Wells was the barrelmaker at the time) and chambered it for the .308 cartridge, and then fitted Blackburn bottom metal to the action. He crafted the stock from a genuine stick of Thessier French walnut and fitted a Biesen trap buttplate to hold all the sight hardware.

PHOTO COURTESY OF D'ARCY ECHOLS

Steve Hughes began this project with a Martin Hagn single-shot action and an octagon barrel with a full integral rib. Ralph Martini did the barrel work. Hughes reshaped the action and lever to contours he preferred. He then milled bases for Talley rings into the quarter-rib on the barrel. The rifle is chambered for the .280 Remington cartridge. Steven stocked the rifle with an excellent stick of English walnut. He checkered the stock in a point pattern at 25 lines per inch, with a mullered border and fitted a steel buttplate. The rifle remains in the white awaiting the client's decision on engraving.

PHOTO BY STEVEN DODD HUGHES

Starting with an original 1885 Winchester Low Wall action, Gunmaker John Mercer fitted a Green Mountain barrel and chambered it for the .22 Long Rifle rimfire cartridge. Mercer then designed a stock for scope use and crafted the stock in a stick of Circassian walnut from Cecil Fredi. He checkered it in a point pattern with mullered border at 24 lines per inch. He also fitted a Lyman tang peep sight, along with the Lyman Small Game 6X period-styled scope.

PHOTO BY JOHN MERCER

This Model 42 Winchester skeet gun has been completely restored to new condition, mostly following the original Winchester styling. Paul Lindke stocked the little pump in a super stick of American black walnut. He shaped the stock following the lines of the original deluxe style grip and fitted a steel grip cap. He checkered the stock, using the original Winchester Pattern "A" carving at 24 lines per inch. Franz Marktl engraved the gun using a lovely scroll pattern.

PHOTO BY TOM ALEXANDER

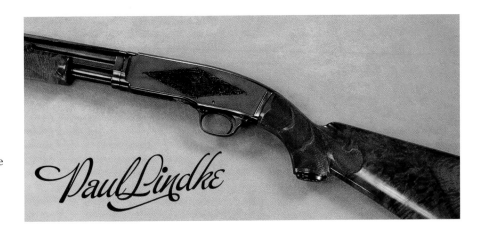

The Winchester Model 21 double shown here was commissioned as a presentation gun for a retiring U.S. Navy SEAL. Paul Lindke was selected to do the stockwork on the project. He started with a very nice stick of Bastogne walnut. He shaped the stock following the lines of original Winchester stocks. To provide for the proper balance, he had to drill three ¾-inch holes in the buttstock to reduce the weight of the wood. With the wood he cut from the buttstock to obtain the proper length of pull, he fashioned three plugs to fill and conceal the holes. The checkering of the butt makes the seams of the plugs totally invisible. Franz Marktl engraved the gun, to include a gold inlaid U.S. Navy SEAL emblem.

PHOTO BY TOM ALEXANDER

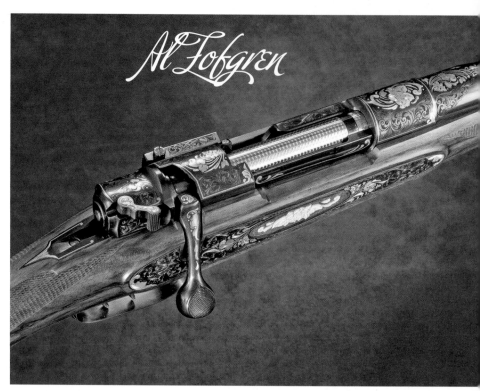

Al Lofgren

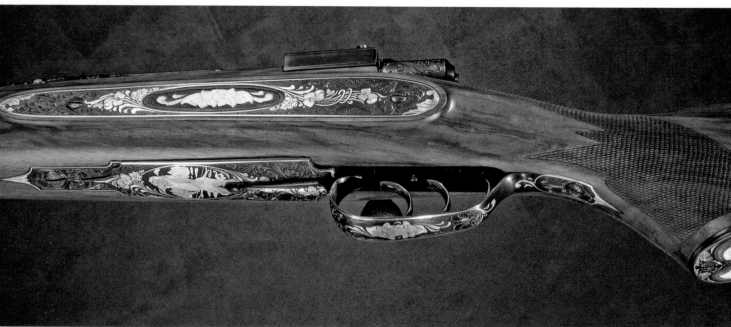

Gunmaker Al Lofgren began this project rifle with a small-ring Mauser '98 action and a blank of excellent California English walnut from the stash of Steve Heilmann. He cleaned up the action, truing all the surfaces, including modification of the rear action tang. He also modified the bottom metal. He then crafted the stock in an early twentieth century styling. He added steel side-plates to the reinforcing areas on either side of the stock, as well as a skeleton buttplate crafted by Glen Fewless.

When the stock was finished, he turned the metalwork over to engraver Brian Hochstradt. Brian then designed and executed the superb engraving, featuring a scene of Diana, Goddess of the Hunt, on the floorplate. Joe Coggin's work inspired his design for the pattern.

Brian also designed the ivory inlays in the stock, which were then carved by Al Lofgren. At the annual American Custom Gunmakers Guild/Firearms Engravers Guild of America combined Exhibition, in Reno, in January 2011, this rifle won the Best Carving Award, Best Engraved Rifle Award, and the Engravers Choice Award.

PHOTO BY TOM ALEXANDER

Mike Dubber

In addition to private clients, Mike Dubber is also a designated Colt Master Engraver, doing work directly for the Colt's custom shop. This magnificent Colt SAA is such a project.

The Colt Collectors Association holds its annual meetings in a different state each year. That state determines the motif for the Grand Auction Gun for that year. In 2009, the state hosting the annual get-together was North Carolina. Most notable of the state's recommendations are the two scrimshaw depictions of the Wright Brothers airplane and the Cape Hatteras Lighthouse on the ivory grips, both executed by Catherine Plumer. Behind the cylinder on the left side of the revolver is a gold inlaid depiction of the battleship USS North Carolina. As an interesting aside, after many years of honorable service, the powers that be scheduled the dismantling of the battleship for scrap, in 1960. The schoolchildren in the North Carolina school system volunteered to donate their lunch money once each week to preserve the state treasure. In the end, the ship was spared, renovated, and now rests in North Carolina waters as a visitor's attraction. Mike did all the engraving and gold inlay work on the "Peacemaker."

PHOTO BY TOM ALEXANDER

Peter Ewalt is a German Master Engraver who studied under my old friend and fantastic engraver, the late Erich Boessler. Peter has been out on his own for many years and is turning out some superb engraving jobs. He did the pre-64 Model 70 floor plate shown here for a good friend (and excellent engraver in his own right), Terry Wilcox.

PHOTO COURTESY OF PETER EWALT

Peter Ewalt

Paula Biesen Malicki

This Kolar 12-bore trap gun was commissioned by a firefighter to honor the actions of the NYC police and fire departments on 9/11. The client chose engraver Paula Biesen-Malicki to execute the engraving. Paula is the daughter of gunmaker Roger Biesen and the granddaughter of an icon in the custom gun trade, Al Biesen. This fine competition gun was custom stocked by Dennis DeVault.

A magnificent 20-bore Parker double, restored to pristine condition and re-stocked in a lovely stick of thin-shelled walnut by Roger Biesen. Roger tapped his daughter, Paula Biesen Malicki, to cut the wonderful engraving pattern on the gun.

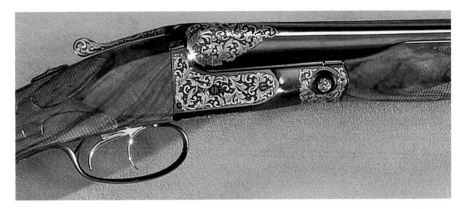

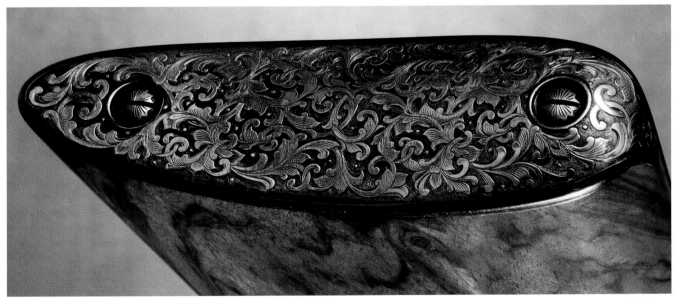

Reto Buehler

This superb double square-bridge Mauser express rifle is from the Oregon shop of Reto Buehler. The client that commissioned its crafting already had a very similar rifle chambered for the .500 Jeffery and wanted a matching rifle chambered for a smaller cartridge. Reto started with a Brno ZG 47 action. He did the normal blueprinting and slicking up the action, including installing a Wisner three-position safety and Blackburn bottom metal. Buehler then installed a Pac-Nor .30-caliber barrel and chambered it for the .30-06 cartridge. He installed a quarter-rib with custom sights, a ramp front sight base, and banded front sling swivel base, then re-milled the integral scope mount bases on the action and extended the tangs on the action and bottom metal.

Next, Reto stocked the rifle in the English style, using a fine piece of Turkish walnut. When finished, he checkered the rifle using flat-topped diamonds and an H&H-style pattern. The rifle is finished with the exception of the final metal finishing and bluing.

Roger Sampson

Engraver Roger Sampson did the exquisite scroll engraving and bulino scenes on this Ruger over/under 28-bore quail gun. Built for a lady, the gun is scaled in the proper proportions to fit the southern belle on her bobwhite quail forays. Al Linde stocked the shotgun. Sampson's work is superb.

PHOTO BY TOM ALEXANDER

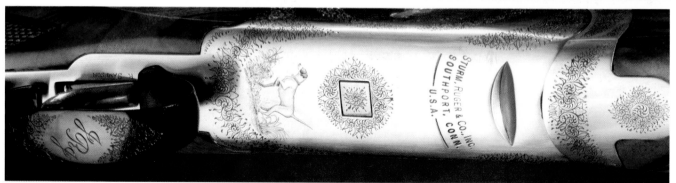

Gene Simillion

PHOTO BY TOM ALEXANDER

Gunmaker Gene Simillion began this project with a GMA Kurz action. GMA fabricated a special magazine box for its action to fit the .223 cartridge. According to Gene, the GMA response when delivering the box was "never again." Simillion fitted a Krieger barrel to the action and installed a quarter-rib with one standing leaf rear sight. He machined the action for Smithson quick-detachable rings, fitted a front barrel band, and color case hardened the safety shroud, grip cap, and rear sling swivel stud. He stocked the rifle with a superb stick of Turkish walnut and checkered it in a point pattern of 26 lines per inch with mullered borders.

Joe Smithson

PHOTO COURTESY OF GENE SIMILLION

Here is Joe Smithson's left-hand .416 Rigby on a GMA action and Krieger over-size barrel blank. He recontoured the factory GMA action and bottom metal to be more to his liking. He then machined the Krieger barrel blank to provide for an integral quarter-rib, front sight base, and front sling swivel stud. He fashioned the stock from a piece of Circassian walnut, fitting a Jerry Fisher grip cap and checkering it in a point pattern of 24 lines per inch with mullered borders. This rifle also features Joe Smithson quick-detachable scope mounts.

PHOTO BY STEVEN DODD HUGHES

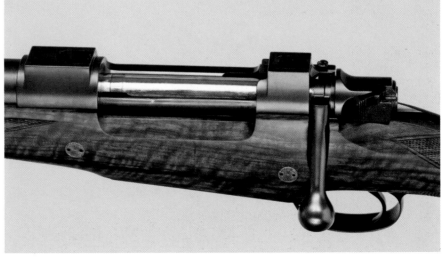

Ryan Breeding

A magnificent .416 Rigby rifle from the shop of Ryan Breeding. Starting with a Granite Mountain Arms double square-bridge magnum Mauser action, Pac Nor barrel, and lovely stick of Turkish walnut, Breeding does the rest in his shop. On this rifle, he fitted a Swarovski Z6 1-6x extended eye relief scope mounted in Talley rings, with bases milled into the double square bridges. Sights and accessories are all shop-made in the Breeding shop.

PHOTO COURTESY OF RYAN BREEDING

This takedown .275 Rigby was built on a Granite Mountain Arms Kurz action fitted with Joe Smithson scope mounts. The barrel is octagonal with integral front sight ramp, sling swivel studs, and quarter-rib by Ralf Martini. Steve Nelson then machined square threads on the barrel to mate up with the special-order square threads in the receiver, chosen to withstand repeated assembly/disassembly; by depressing a button in the fore-end escutcheon, the barrel unscrews from the action. Nelson then made a stock pattern to precisely fit the client and then machined a lovely stick of exhibition grade walnut using the pattern. After finishing with many coats of hand-rubbed oil, he checkered the stock with a fleur-de-lis ribbon pattern designed just for this client.

Bob Evans then executed the engraving duties. Since the client is of Norse ancestry, the designs were all taken from Norse mythology, and the gold runes on the quarter-rib are the client's initials. After Evans finished the engraving, George Komadina rust blued the metalwork. Evans then selectively French grayed the engraving.

Bob Evans

When the rifle was finished, but before engraving, the client just had to take his rifle on a moose hunt in Sweden where he dropped a nice bull on the first morning with a single, well-placed shot. A good omen!

PHOTOS BY TOM ALEXANDER

Roger Biesen

These two images are of the first Jack O'Connor Commemorative Rifle. Roger Biesen crafted the rifle in the same style as his father, Al, had done, in 1959, to Jack's favorite rife of all time. I believe Al, who is now past 90 years of age, did quite a bit of "supervising" on the build of this rifle. A third-generation Biesen, Roger's daughter Paula Biesen-Malicki, engraved Jack's best ram, the Pilot Mountain ram, on the buttplate.

PHOTOS COURTESY OF THE BIESEN FAMILY

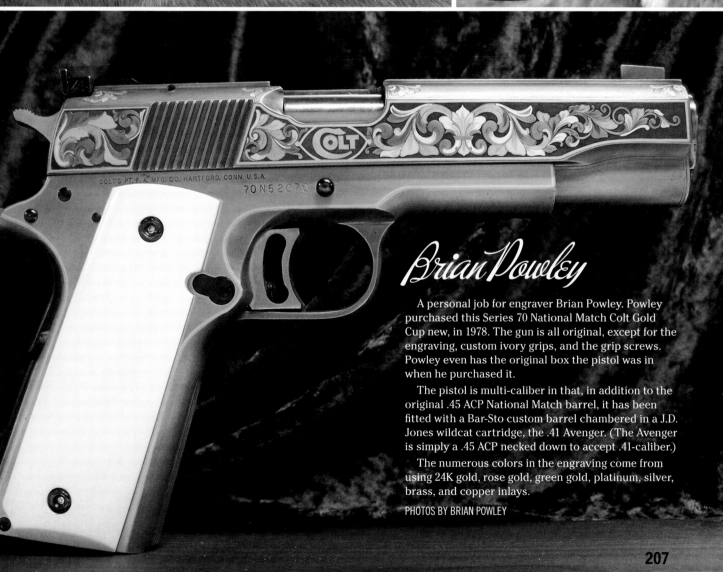

Brian Powley

A personal job for engraver Brian Powley. Powley purchased this Series 70 National Match Colt Gold Cup new, in 1978. The gun is all original, except for the engraving, custom ivory grips, and the grip screws. Powley even has the original box the pistol was in when he purchased it.

The pistol is multi-caliber in that, in addition to the original .45 ACP National Match barrel, it has been fitted with a Bar-Sto custom barrel chambered in a J.D. Jones wildcat cartridge, the .41 Avenger. (The Avenger is simply a .45 ACP necked down to accept .41-caliber.)

The numerous colors in the engraving come from using 24K gold, rose gold, green gold, platinum, silver, brass, and copper inlays.

PHOTOS BY BRIAN POWLEY

207

Mike Dubber

I haven't spoken with Mike Dubber about this commission, but I'd wager a king's ransom that it was done for a native Kentuckian. Dubber embellished this Colt Bisley Flat-Top model exquisitely, with scroll, gold inlay, and carved ivory grips. As the TV commercial once said, "It just doesn't get any better than this."

PHOTOS BY SAM WELCH

This rifle was crafted, at the instructions of the client, for a specific task. It was designed to be a treestand gun! The client wanted a technically perfect rifle of the highest quality, but he wanted no glitz or glamour. Custom maker Dave Norin set about accomplishing the instructions by selecting a 1908 Brazilian Mauser action. He blueprinted the action, installed a Model 70-type three-position safety, and installed a .30-caliber barrel that he chambered for the .30-06 cartridge. He fitted Ted Blackburn bottom metal with the Oberndorf-style trigger guard bow to the action. He then stocked it with a piece of excellent, but very plain, walnut. The client, and this writer believes he succeeded admirably.

Dave Norin

Starting with a VZ-24 Mauser action and a Krieger barrel, custom maker Dave Norin crafted this wonderfully lightweight deer rifle. He used Fisher rounded bottom metal, a Biesen buttplate, and a Fisher grip cap and crafted the stock with a very nice stick of English walnut. He checkered the stock with a point pattern featuring a mullered border at 22 lines per inch. Ken Hurst did the engraving.

PHOTOS BY TOM ALEXANDER

This lovely custom Dakota Model 10 belongs to my colleague and friend Terry Wieland. In addition to being a fantastically talented writer, Terry is also a connoisseur of fine firearms, particularly rifles. This Dakota is no exception. Starting with a Model 10 action and .25-caliber barrel from Dakota, a magnificent stock blank from Bill Dowtin of Old World Walnut, a grip cap and sling swivels from Brownells, and a set of Talley scope bases and rings from Gary Turner of Talley Manu-facturing, Terry delivered the goods to Master custom maker James Flynn. Flynn did all the stock and metal work on this rifle, with the exception of the superb case coloring and bluing. That specialized talent was entrusted to Doug Turnbull. Chambered for the .250/3000 Savage cartridge, it is Terry's idea of what a fine single-shot rifle should look like.

As an interesting aside, the blank from which James Flynn crafted the stock (using chisels, rasps, and other hand tools, with no machine-shaping involved), came from the Caucasus Mountains, the source of true Circas-sian walnut. Bill Dowtin related that, on a trip to the area, he came across a little man, in Georgia, that had cut up a tree using a chainsaw. Dowtin bought three blanks from him, all from the root section below ground level. The tree was estimated to be a minimum of 300 years old.

PHOTOS BY TERRY WIELAND

Terry Wieland

Gary Stiles

This fine rifle began life as a factory Remington Model 700 chambered for the .30-06 cartridge. Custom Maker Gary Stiles then cleaned up the metalwork and added a Model 70-type safety, a set of Dakota bottom metal, and checkered the bolt knob. Using a nice stick of Turkish walnut from Luxus Walnut, he fashioned the excellent custom stock, adding Talley sling swivel bases, a Dakota skeleton grip cap, an ebony fore-end tip with widow's peak, a bearskin covered recoil pad, and checkered the stock in a 24 lines per inch wraparound pattern with ribbons. He then mounted a Leupold VXIII 2.5-8x variable power scope in Talley mounts. Engraver Ron Nott completed the job with his tasteful scroll engraving.

PHOTOS COURTESY OF GARY STILES

This superb "Kentucky" flintlock rifle was made entirely by hand by Hugh Toenjes. He started the stock with a square blank of curly maple and fashioned the stock fully by hand. No stock duplicator or other high-tech machinery was used. He finished the stock by hand rubbing a combination of various stains, boiled linseed oil, tung oil, and Japan dryers. This finishing alone took three weeks to complete.

All the brass furniture was crafted from solid stock, primarily using a file and hacksaw. The two exceptions are the trigger guard and butt plate, which were fashioned from rough sand castings.

Using a rough octagon barrel blank that had only been deep drilled, Toenjes rifled it by hand, using his own style. He honed it to his specifications, filed a breech plug from solid stock, and fitted it to the barrel. After proof firing the barrel for accuracy, which produced several five-shot groups measuring 1¼ inches at 100 yards, he draw-filed the flats to the final dimensions, ready for inletting.

Toenjes made the lock from a combination of rough castings and springs filed out by hand. Toenjes also did all the stock decoration, as well as all the metal engraving.

This exquisite rifle is a wonderful example of Old World craftsmanship and talent.

ALL PHOTOS BY ROBERT FOGT PHOTOGRAPHY

211

This very nice "Southpaw" rifle is from the shop of Robert Mercer. Mercer built the gun for a very special purpose, not for a client, but as a gift for his son. He started the project with a Montana 1999 action and a Krieger barrel. He fitted the 7mm barrel to the action and chambered it for the .280 Ackley Improved cartridge.

Robert Mercer

He then stocked the rifle in a very nice stick of English walnut and checkered it in a 26 lines per inch fleur-de-lis pattern. Finally, he mounted a Leupold scope in Talley rings and bases. Jerome Glimm did the lovely engraving. Mercer told me that, since he finished the rifle and gave it to his son, their target bill has gone down considerably. The rifle seems to consistently deliver nothing bigger than ½-MOA groups. PHOTOS BY TOM ALEXANDER

Lee Griffiths

Al Lofgren

Starting with a post-war FN large-ring action, Al Lofgren set about crafting a fine .30-06 hunting rifle. Dave Norin did all the metalwork on the rifle, including fitting a McFarland checkered bolt knob and Talley scope mounts. Lofgren crafted the stock from a nice stick of English walnut. He fitted a skeleton grip cap and butt plate to the stock, but filled the openings with ebony inlays, which he checkered. A superb and unusual job.

PHOTOS BY TOM ALEXANDER

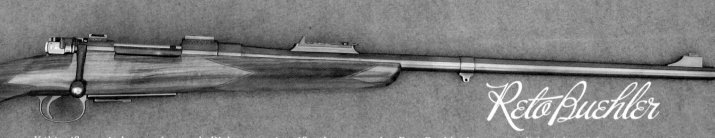

Reto Buehler

If this rifle reminds you of an early Rigby magazine rifle, then gunmaker Reto Buehler has accomplished the job he set out to do. He started with a Steyr M98 Mauser action. At the time, he had in the shop a 1910 Oberndorf Mauser built for Rigby, so he copied the barrel contour in a new Pad Nor 9.3mm barrel, and Reto fitted the new barrel to the action and chambered it for the 9.3x62 cartridge. He added the square bridges to the action, as well as Recknagel side-swing scope mounts. To the barrel, he shop-made and added an express and ladder rear sight, just like the original Rigby. He retained the original military magazine box, but added a straddle-type floorplate to which he built in a hinged lever floorplate release. While it is a new rifle, it is very reminiscent of the early 1900 products. A very masterful job.

PHOTOS BY RETO BUEHLER

Engraver Lee Griffiths, responding to general guidelines from a client, came up with this design for engraving the client's Perazzi shotgun. According to Lee, the client suggested bugs, stinging, nasty bugs on each side, and butterflies on the bottom. Lee admitted that the spider on the break-lever was his idea.

When I asked him how he came up with the design, he told me, "Eat enough spicy foods and have enough bad nightmares, and you can come up with stuff like this!" Perhaps not everyone's taste in design, the execution is marvelously done. This job won the Engravers Choice Merit award at the 2009 FEGA/ACGG combined Exhibition.

PHOTOS BY SAM WELCH

One of the premiere gunmakers in the world is D'Arcy Echols. His work with bolt-action rifles is among the finest on this planet. Not the most extravagant, not the flashiest, and not the most attention-getting, mind you, but he is among a handful of the very best artisans building rifles.

Echols began work on this rifle with a Winchester Model 70 Classic action, which was completely reworked in the Echols shop. A 7mm barrel was then fitted to the action and chambered for the 7mm Remington Magnum cartridge. All the accessories—bottom metal, scope mounts, sling swivels and studs, etc.—are all custom made in the Echols shop. Echols then crafted a superb stock from excellent, but not ornate, English walnut. The final task was fitting a Schmidt & Bender 3-12x Zenith scope to the rifle in Echols mounts.

PHOTOS COURTESY OF D'ARCY ECHOLS

D'Arcy Echols

This wonderful double rifle is a No. 11 Jeffery's Express Rifle, chambered for the .475 No. 2 Cordite cartridge. It features Krupp steel barrels, 24 inches in length. It is a non-ejector rifle and weighs 11½ pounds. From all indications, it was manufactured between 1907 and 1909. The rifle has been completely reconditioned and restocked to "as new" condition.

The metalwork was completely restored by Pete Mazur. All metal parts were reconditioned and refinished using proper period finishes. The engraving was recut, as required.

Darwin Hensley, one of our very best stockers, restocked the rifle. The blank that Hensley selected is a stick of exhibition grade Turkish walnut of exceptional quality, and the styling of the stock is distinctively Hensley's.

Of special note, Mazur custom fitted an original Purdey folding peep sight to the barrels. The owner of the rifle now shoots 1½-inch groups at 25 yards instead of the previous eight-inch groups using the "normal" leaf sights.

PHOTOS BY TOM ALEXANDER

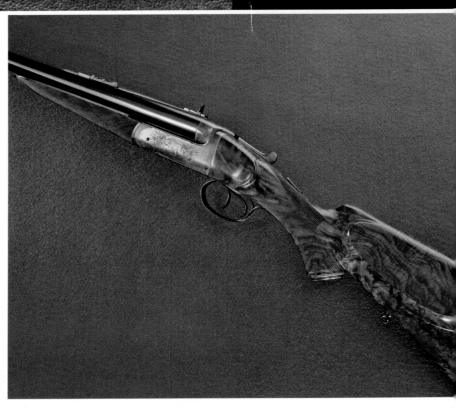

This fine pair of rifles was crafted to support the American Custom Gunmakers Guild Foundation. Larry Potterfield, of MidwayUSA, started the process by donating two consecutively serial numbered Remington Model 700 short actions. Douglas then donated two air-gauged chrome moly barrels, one in .222 and the other in .257. Fred Wenig donated two Bastogne walnut stock blanks, and Leupold followed with two 4-12x variable power scopes, also with consecutive serial numbers. John Maxson did the stocks, including checkering each in a 20 lines per inch border-less checkering pattern. Brian Powley did the modest engraving on the rifles.

PHOTOS BY TOM ALEXANDER

John Maxson

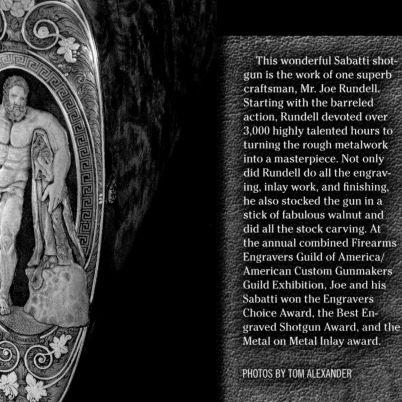

Joe Rundell

This wonderful Sabatti shotgun is the work of one superb craftsman, Mr. Joe Rundell. Starting with the barreled action, Rundell devoted over 3,000 highly talented hours to turning the rough metalwork into a masterpiece. Not only did Rundell do all the engraving, inlay work, and finishing, he also stocked the gun in a stick of fabulous walnut and did all the stock carving. At the annual combined Firearms Engravers Guild of America/American Custom Gunmakers Guild Exhibition, Joe and his Sabatti won the Engravers Choice Award, the Best Engraved Shotgun Award, and the Metal on Metal Inlay award.

PHOTOS BY TOM ALEXANDER

Steve Heilmann

Bob Snapp

This very unusual rifle is the combination of several highly talented artisans. Bob Snapp did the metalwork on the Martini barreled action. Though Bob can do metalwork on any firearm, he is most at home working on single-shot rifles like this Martini. Kent Bowerly fashioned the stock from a magnificent stick of crotch-grain walnut and carried out the unique checkering pattern. Bob Evans then designed and executed the one-of-a-kind engraving pattern. All of the symbols are from the Kwakiutl Indian tribe of coastal southwest British Columbia.

PHOTOS BY TOM ALEXANDER

This single-shot 7mm STW features the metalwork of Steve Heilmann, the engraving of Denis Reece, the bluing and finishing of Pete Mazur, the color case hardening of Doug Turnbull, and the stockwork of Keith Heppler. The action used is a Hagn. The rifle exhibits marvelous work from a group of superb artisans.

PHOTOS BY TOM ALEXANDER

217

Mike Roden

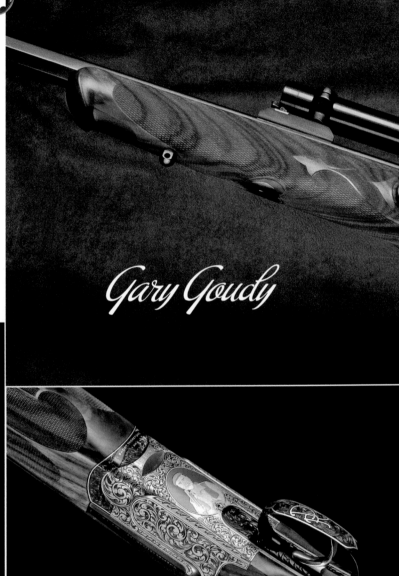

In the gun above, Granite Mountain Arms set out to replicate the century-old technology that produced the Mauser action, but using modern CNC equipment. In the early days, Mike Roden leaned heavily on the late Fred Wells for advice, and today, the Granite Mountain Arms Mauser action is one of the finest available. Machined from 8620 steel, it is hell's own for strong. Currently available in short magnum, standard magnum, express magnum, and the massive African magnum, rumor has it that we'll soon see a modern recreation of the G33/40 Mauser action. The rifle shown here is a .458 Lott built on the Express magnum action. The metalwork is by Granite Mountain Arms, the stock by Joe Smithson, and the exquisite engraving by Mark Swanson.

PHOTOS COURTESY OF GRANITE MOUNTAIN ARMS

Gary Goudy

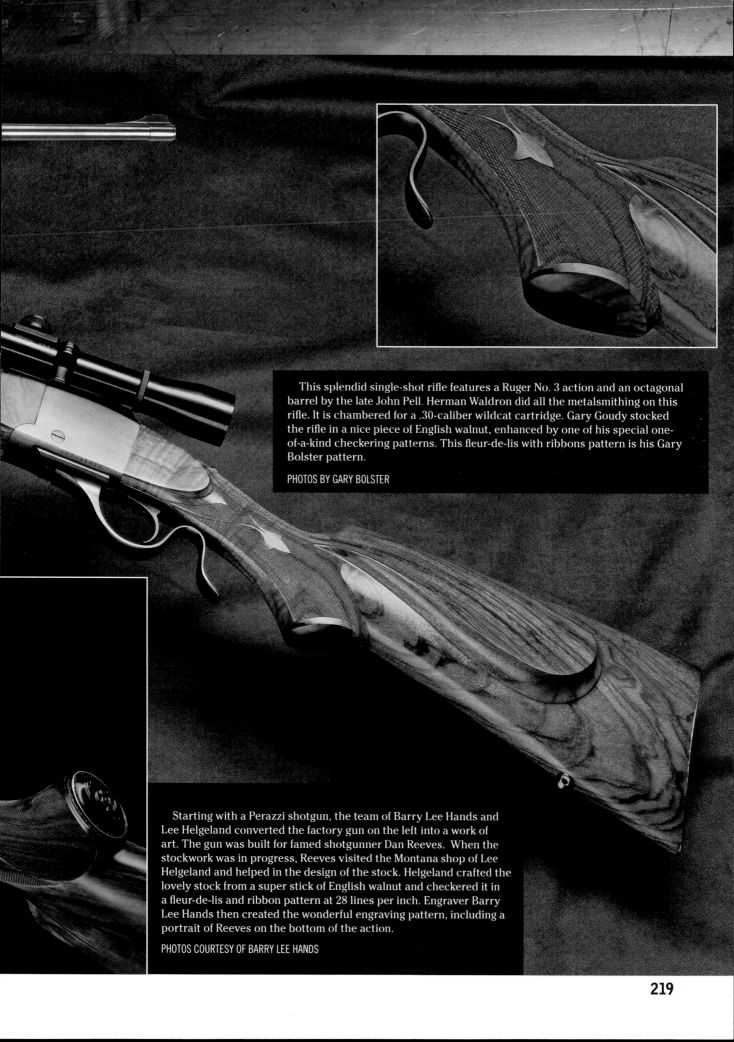

This splendid single-shot rifle features a Ruger No. 3 action and an octagonal barrel by the late John Pell. Herman Waldron did all the metalsmithing on this rifle. It is chambered for a .30-caliber wildcat cartridge. Gary Goudy stocked the rifle in a nice piece of English walnut, enhanced by one of his special one-of-a-kind checkering patterns. This fleur-de-lis with ribbons pattern is his Gary Bolster pattern.

PHOTOS BY GARY BOLSTER

Starting with a Perazzi shotgun, the team of Barry Lee Hands and Lee Helgeland converted the factory gun on the left into a work of art. The gun was built for famed shotgunner Dan Reeves. When the stockwork was in progress, Reeves visited the Montana shop of Lee Helgeland and helped in the design of the stock. Helgeland crafted the lovely stock from a super stick of English walnut and checkered it in a fleur-de-lis and ribbon pattern at 28 lines per inch. Engraver Barry Lee Hands then created the wonderful engraving pattern, including a portrait of Reeves on the bottom of the action.

PHOTOS COURTESY OF BARRY LEE HANDS

Caesar Guerini

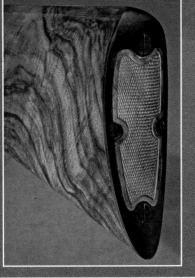

The gun below is one of a pair of George Gibbs Farquharson rifles in the process of being restored by Trez Hensley, of Hensley and Hensley Gun Works. This rifle is chambered for the .450/400 Nitro Express cartridge, and Ralf Martini did the barrel. Trez then crafted the fabulous stock from a stick of superb Turkish walnut. He checkered it at 26 lines per inch. Next step on the stock is to leather-cover the recoil pad. The original factory engraving has been maintained, and still to be done is the case coloring of the action and bluing of the barrel.

PHOTOS BY STEVEN DODD HUGHES

George Gibbs

This beautiful big-game rifle started with a Johannsen magnum Mauser action and a Krieger 375 H&H barrel. The action is fitted a Swarovski scope mounted in Joe Smithson quick-detach scope mounts. Lee Helgeland executed the metalwork on the rifle, and Barry Lee Hands engraved it. Gary Goudy stocked the rifle in a piece of Thessier French walnut, which he says is the oldest piece of walnut he has ever used. It was cut sometime in the 1920s. He checkered the stock in a fastidious point pattern. The owner of this rifle, by the way, owns a cherry orchard, explaining the unusual inlay on the floorplate.

PHOTOS BY GARY BOLSTER

This Caesar Guerini over/under 20-bore shotgun, with an extra set of 28-bore barrels, was delivered to Al Lind for one of his exquisite stock jobs. Bill Dowtin of Old World Walnut supplied the superlative blank of Circassian walnut, and Al whittled it into this lovely stock. He also fitted the stock with an elegant skeleton buttplate. The result is the lovely gun shown here.

PHOTOS BY TOM ALEXANDER

Terry Wieland

This rifle was built for Gray's Sporting Journal Shooting Editor Terry Wieland. Terry is a lover of fine guns, particularly period-style pieces. This is just such a rifle. It is chambered for the .40-70 Straight Sharps cartridge, has a 34-inch octagonal barrel, and is fitted with target sights provided by Brownells. The barrel work was done by Danny Pedersen of Classic Barrel & Gunworks. The stock was crafted by Robert Szweda from a superb blank of Circassian walnut supplied by Bill Dowtin of Old World Walnut, while the action was accent-engraved by Sam Welch. Finally, the action was case hardened, the barrel blued, and the final fitting done by Doug Turnbull of Turnbull Restoration. All this work was performed on a Ruger No. 1 action.

PHOTOS BY TOM ALEXANDER

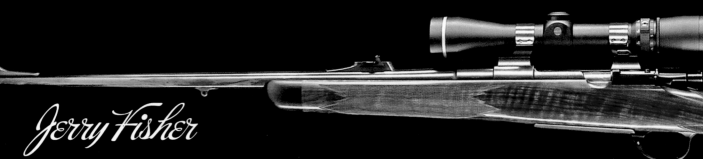

Jerry Fisher

All work, wood, and metal on this rifle is from the old master Jerry Fisher. The Mauser action has been trued and fitted with a three-position safety shroud. The Leupold scope is mounted in Joe Smithson detachable scope mounts, and Jerry fitted his Fisher rounded-bottom metal to the action. Fisher fashioned the purely classically designed stock from a blank of fine and superb European walnut. He fitted a steel buttplate and checkered the stock in a stylish point pattern with mullered borders. This .30-06 reeks of classic elegance.

PHOTOS COURTESY OF BARRY LEE HANDS

Chuck Grace started this rifle with a 1909 Argentine Mauser that had been metalsmithed by the great Tom Burgess. Joe Smithson made the fantastic scope mounting system, and Gary Griffiths did the engraving. Chuck did the rest, including the metalwork on the barrel. He whittled out the superb stock from a stick of English walnut, checkered it in an elegant point pattern, and fitted it with a trap buttplate. Topped off with a Leupold scope, this .30-06 is ready to go hunting.

PHOTOS BY TOM ALEXANDER

Chuck Grace

Brian Hochstrat

A marvelous Colt SAA from the shop of Brian Hochstrat. Starting with a 3rd Generation, 7½-inch barrel Colt, chambered for the .32-20 cartridge, Brian spent 330 hours lavishly engraving and gold inlaying the pistol. He also fashioned the ivory grips for the piece. It is a wonderful example of the engraver's art.

PHOTOS BY TOM ALEXANDER

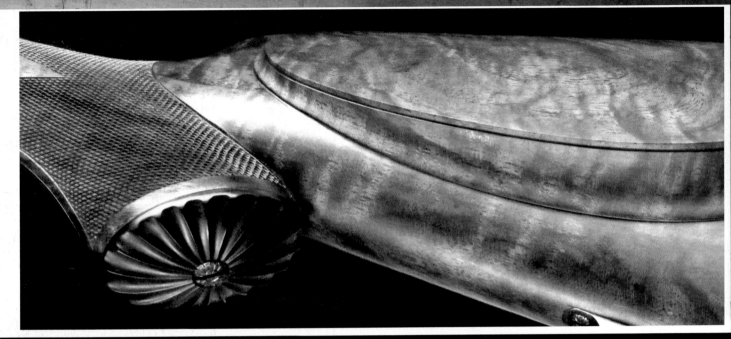

This unusual and seldom seen single-shot rifle is from the Montana shop of Lee Helgeland. The rifle project began when Lee acquired the Schmidt-Habermann—sometimes called a Kettner—action quite a number of years ago. Rick Stickley did the barrel work about 15 years ago, which included milling an integral quarter-rib and front sight ramp, as well as a sling swivel base. He chambered the barrel for the 7x57R cartridge and fitted the barrel to the action. Lee reshaped the action and lever for a better look and fashioned a set of scope rings for the rifle from a set of "gunmaker" rings out of Germany. He then crafted the beautiful stock from a stick of Turkish walnut, fitted a genuine horn buttplate, grip cap, and fore-end tip to the stock, checkered it in a borderless pattern 28 lines per inch, and gold-plated all the internal parts.

PHOTOS BY STEVEN DODD HUGHES

Lee Helgeland

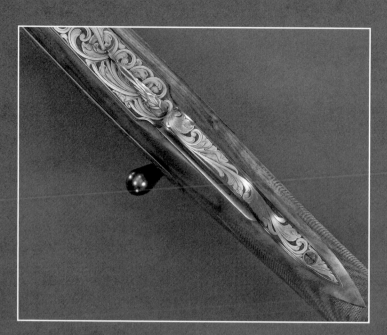

This full-stocked rifle, a lá Mannlicher, is from the shop of Al Lofgren. Starting with a Swedish Mauser action, custom barreled for the 6.5x55 cartridge, Lofgren turned it into this lovely custom rifle. Very Germanic in styling, to include the double-set trigger and stock carvings, it exemplifies the Teutonic styling. Al did all the stockwork, to include the carving; Dave Norin did most of the metalwork; and Brian Hochstrat did the engraving.

PHOTOS BY TOM ALEXANDER

Brian Hochstrat

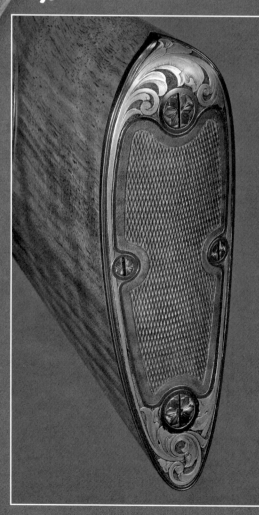

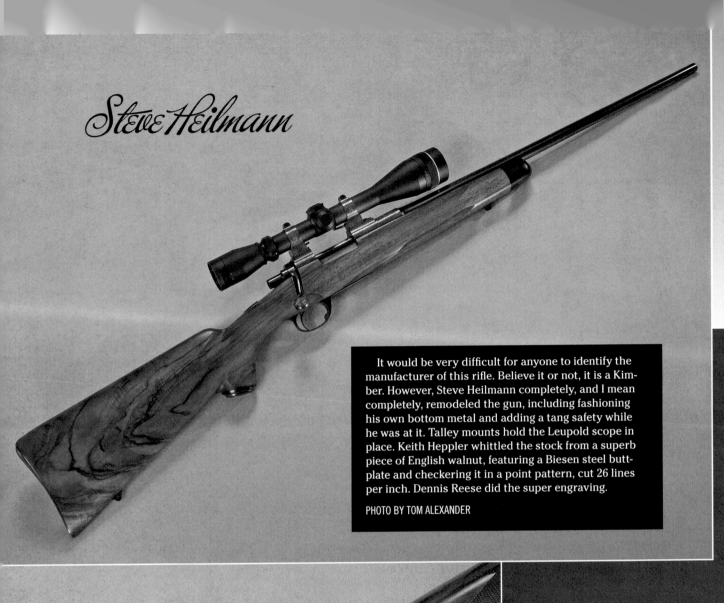

Steve Heilmann

It would be very difficult for anyone to identify the manufacturer of this rifle. Believe it or not, it is a Kimber. However, Steve Heilmann completely, and I mean completely, remodeled the gun, including fashioning his own bottom metal and adding a tang safety while he was at it. Talley mounts hold the Leupold scope in place. Keith Heppler whittled the stock from a superb piece of English walnut, featuring a Biesen steel buttplate and checkering it in a point pattern, cut 26 lines per inch. Dennis Reese did the super engraving.

PHOTO BY TOM ALEXANDER

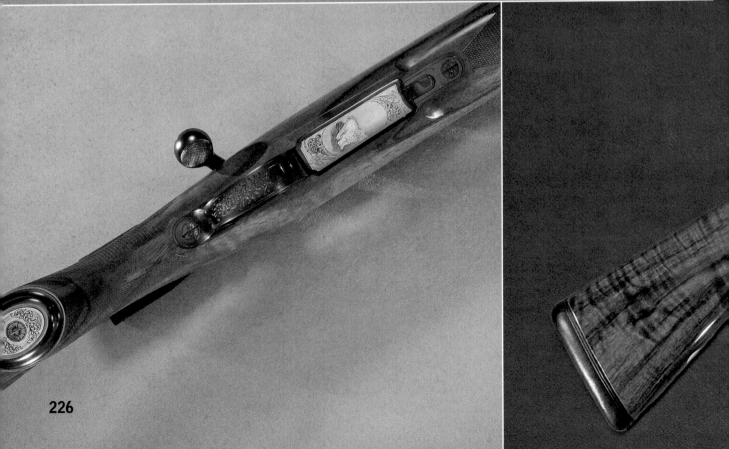

Shane Thompson

ABOVE: Shane Thompson built this rifle for himself as his hunting rifle. He started with a commercial Mauser action. He fitted and recontoured a Douglas XX barrel and chambered it for the 280 Remington cartridge. He did extensive metalwork to the action including making custom rings and bases, and a custom floorplate. He fashioned a sculpted safety button and checkered it. He did all the finish work, including rust bluing the metalwork and added nitre-blued accents. Shane stocked his rifle with a stick of English walnut, and checkered it in a 24 lines-per-inch point pattern with mullered border. The finished rifle weighs 8 pounds with scope. To date, it has accounted for an Alaskan moose, two caribou, two black bears and a nice four-point mule deer buck.
PHOTO BY EUGENE WRIGHT

Dale Tate

This lovely double shotgun originated as an AYA sidelock barreled action in-the-white. Dale Tate, articled at Purdey as an actioner, rebuilt the gun in the Purdey likeness. Charles Lee, articled at Purdey as an engraver, executed the lovely scroll engraving on the gun. Dennis Earl Smith did all the stockwork, finished it in oil, and checkered it 24 lines per inch. The client for this fine gun loves it and uses it in the field.

PHOTO BY TOM ALEXANDER

227

MOSSBERG 835

Waterfowlers encounter mud, ice, water, and a world of other harsh conditions every day. The 835 Ulti-Mag Waterfowler from Mossberg is the pump shotgun that can take it all and still fill limits. This isn't just a standard 3-inch shotgun stretched to take the longer 3½-inch shell. Nope, Mossberg specially sized the bolt face, receiver and other necessary components just for the longest 12-gauge shell, ensuring maximum performance and accuracy. They also get their barrels over-bored to 10-gauge dimensions, which optimizes patterning and reduces recoil on the magnum loads.

SPORTING SHOTGUNS

My oh my how things have changed over the decades. When I got into the gun business in the early 1990s, sporting shotguns, for the first time in a long time, were undergoing a revolution of sorts. I distinctly remember the debut of Browning's Gold semi-automatic and its "speed-feed" feature, whereby a shell loaded into the magazine of an otherwise empty gun would be automatically fed up into the receiver and chambered. I bought one of the first ones to hit the shelves then, long before the gun was introduced in a 3½-inch version.

I also remember the introduction of Benelli's Super Black Eagle and the price tag it bore, more than a thousand dollars—and for a semi-auto at that! The gun store I worked for at the time couldn't keep them in stock. Must have been the harbinger of things to come, for a grand is often the starting point for today's myriad semi-auto firearms.

To be sure, these hefty price tags, which used to be preserved for two-barreled shotguns, are due in part to some real innovations and the inclusion of features that used to be reserved for upgraded options. We've seen the creativeness of Benelli's Inertia Driven System, which is shared by the Franchi and Stoeger semi-automatics, Browning's Power Drive System and its improved piston design, the foundation for the Maxus line of shotguns, and Beretta's Blink operating system that makes its semi-autos some of the fastest out there. Then there are features like lengthened forcing cones, extended choke tubes in sets of five instead of the old standard of three flush tubes, multiple recoil reduction points, length-of-pull shim kits, and adjustable cheekpieces. Many of these features used to cost you a lot to upgrade to, or you were going to have to find a gunsmith to make stock and forcing cone adjustments. Couple these things with the exploding sport of 3-gun competition and its specialty shotguns from makers like Benelli and FNH USA, and about the only things these guns don't do is load themselves and make you coffee in the morning.

Even over/unders, the haloed two-barrel choice of American shotgunners, who have never grabbed onto the side-by-sides the Europeans still grasp, has seen its share of innovations. Most of this has been in the guns intended for rigorous competition, primarily the sporting clays crowd. Where before the racks of guns for the sport were split between the relatively affordable Brownings and Berettas on one end and the Krieghoffs and Perazzis on the other, makers like Blaser and Geurini offer competition-ready, star-quality over/under clay guns in the middle ground price ranges. Wes Lang, of Caesar Geurini, told me when we visited at the 2012 SHOT show, that, in general, hunting guns for many makers are at a standstill, while guns oriented for the games are flying off the shelves.

That's an interesting observation, and while some will grab their catalogs of statistics and say its due to global warming, the melting ice cap, the grouse cycle being out of whack, and an irregular number of tornados causing a mass exodus of hunters transitioning over to the clay sports, I don't think it's anything as readily tangible as that. Rather, I think it's a comment on the state of shotguns themselves.

Today's hunting shotguns are feature-laden, ultra-reliable, and offer more functional variety than ever before (i.e., the ever-increasing number of pellet-throwers that chamber and cycle everything from 7/8-inch target loads up through the entire spectrum of 3½-inch magnums). Too, you no longer need one gun for pheasants and another for turkey hunting. Swap out a barrel, swap out a stock, take out a shim spacer so the gun fits over your turkey vest, and voila! One gun can truly do it all, with minimal investment, and that investment will last you until there's nothing left to shoot in this world but the cockroaches.

As for the uptick in the sales for competition-type guns? Well, gamers will always be gamers, and they will always look for the next gun that will put more "Xs" on the score sheet. Nobody gets serious about playing the clay games or 3-gun or even cowboy action shooting without plunking down the dollars, and more guns are always better than fewer for shooting, thus, there's a steady stream of dollars injected into guns that fit these genres. It also helps that TV shows like *3-Gun Nation* and *Hot Shots* have an enormous following and are getting folks interested in the shooting sports who would otherwise never have considered including a firearms in their lives or homes.

Does this mean hunting guns have come to a standstill? Probably not. Televised hunting shows, formerly relegated to a few stations on the upper reaches of your Dish or Direct TV menu, are now seeing mainstream popularity, with shows like *Hogs Gone Wild* on the Discovery Channel, *American Hoggers* and the new *Duck Dynasty* on A&E, and *Swamp People* on the History Channel, to name a few. Oh, and let's not forget about the trending preppers community (*Doomsday Preppers* on NatGeo channel and *Doomsday Bunkers* on Discovery), rife with both tactical and sporting guns that'll put food on the table and defend against whatever evil will remain when the world goes to H-E-Double-Toothpick and we're all off the grid. Together, these "reality" shows are somewhat in the vein of the very successful *Dirty Jobs*, which gave everyone a look behind the scenes of hundreds of jobs that go on around each and every one of us every day. *Dirty Jobs* both normalized and glorified the careers of trash collectors, cheese makers, and mule-driving tree loggers, and it appears that maybe *Swamp People* and *Duck Dynasty* (you can get rich shooting ducks—yahoo!) may do the same for those of us who hunt. And couldn't we gun owners use a little bit of normalizing and glorifying?

—*Jennifer L.S. Pearsall, Editor, Gun Digest Books*

BROWNING CITORI TRAP LEFT-HAND

Browning's Citori XT Trap 12-gauge comes with 30- or 32-inch tubes, HIVIZ ProComp fiber optics, and stretched forcing cones, and left-handed shooters have a version cast just for them. Straight runs of 25 are nothing but a walk in the park.

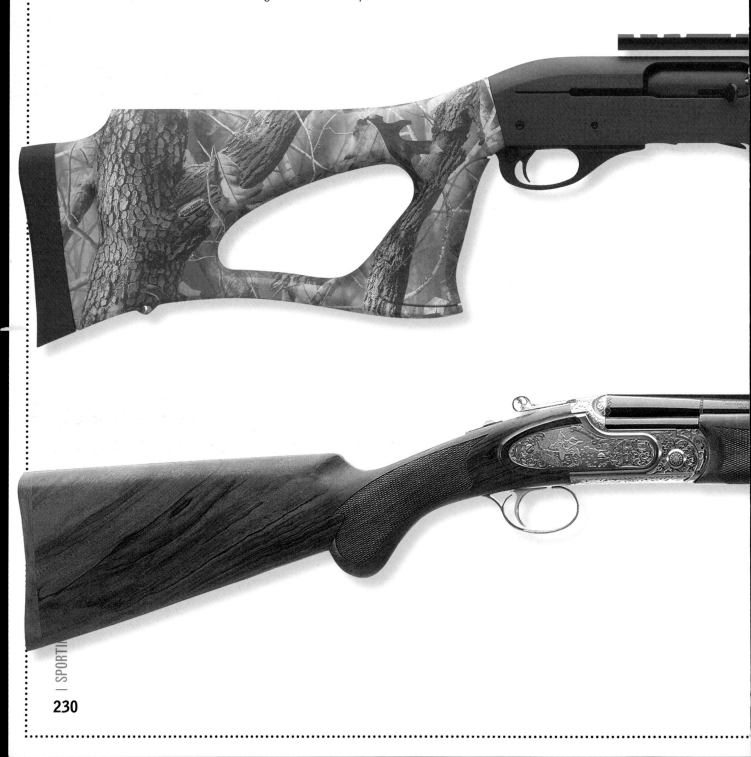

REMINGTON 1187 SURESHOT CANTILEVER

Love slugs for deer hunting? Remington's 11-87 Sportsman Shurshot Camo Cantilever is prime for mounting a low-powered scope, and the thumbhole stock ensures a dead-on hold when the big one walks up.

BENELLI VELOCE

The Veloce SP 20-gauge over/under from Benelli, is a classy, gorgeous example of its Italian heritage, and at just 5½ pounds is a beautifully swinging choice for quail, woodcock, and grouse.

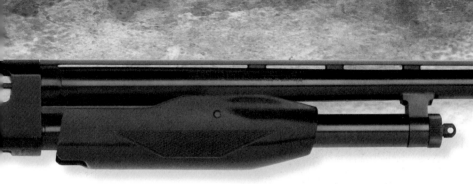

MOSSBERG 510 MINI BANTAM

Kids outgrow their guns as fast as they do their clothes. Mossberg's 510 Mini Bantam and its add-it-as-they-grow stock lengthener inserts keep a shooting sports-obsessed kid going without stripping your budget. In 20-gauge or .410-bore.

REMINGTON 1100 COMPETITION

The Remington 1100 Competition gives clay games shooters the field gun they love tweaked to bust orange discs, with an optional adjustable stock and cheek-piece, overbored 30-inch barrel, extended Briley target chokes, and an in-stock recoil reducing system.

REMINGTON VERSA MAX

It's the little things that sometimes make a gun worth buying. For waterfowlers, it's the rubber grip inserts on Remington's Versa Max semi-auto shotgun that cycles any 12-gauge load to 3½-inches without skipping a beat. These textured add-ons sure help a hunter stay in the swing of things in slick, wet conditions.

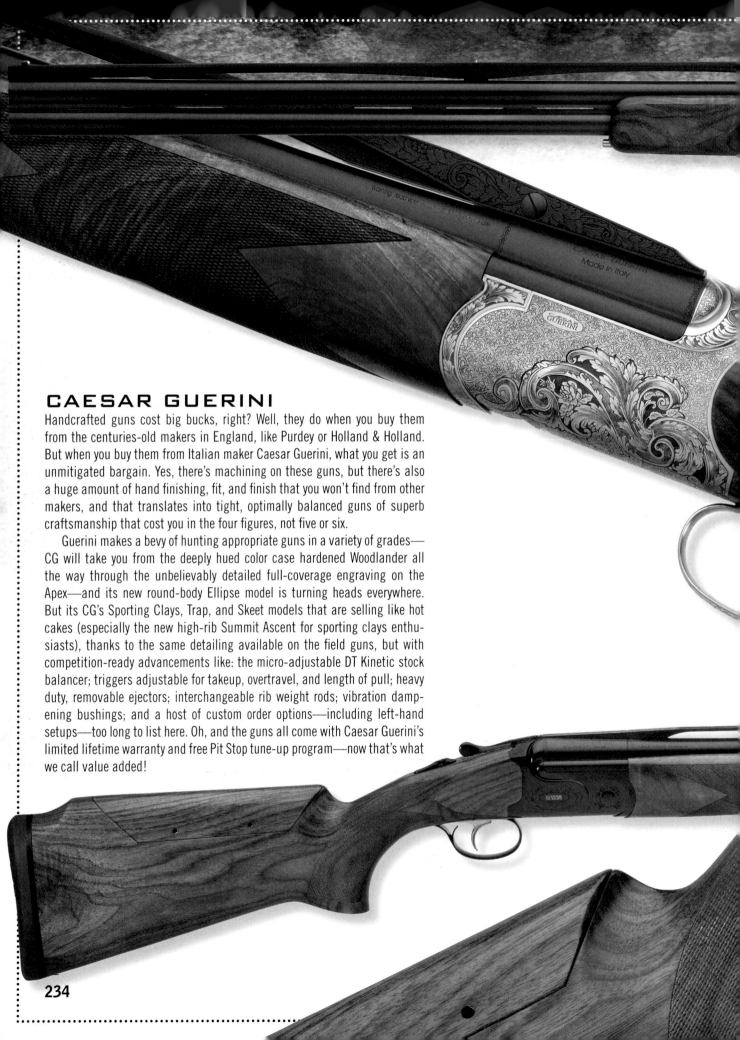

CAESAR GUERINI

Handcrafted guns cost big bucks, right? Well, they do when you buy them from the centuries-old makers in England, like Purdey or Holland & Holland. But when you buy them from Italian maker Caesar Guerini, what you get is an unmitigated bargain. Yes, there's machining on these guns, but there's also a huge amount of hand finishing, fit, and finish that you won't find from other makers, and that translates into tight, optimally balanced guns of superb craftsmanship that cost you in the four figures, not five or six.

Guerini makes a bevy of hunting appropriate guns in a variety of grades— CG will take you from the deeply hued color case hardened Woodlander all the way through the unbelievably detailed full-coverage engraving on the Apex—and its new round-body Ellipse model is turning heads everywhere. But its CG's Sporting Clays, Trap, and Skeet models that are selling like hot cakes (especially the new high-rib Summit Ascent for sporting clays enthusiasts), thanks to the same detailing available on the field guns, but with competition-ready advancements like: the micro-adjustable DT Kinetic stock balancer; triggers adjustable for takeup, overtravel, and length of pull; heavy duty, removable ejectors; interchangeable rib weight rods; vibration dampening bushings; and a host of custom order options—including left-hand setups—too long to list here. Oh, and the guns all come with Caesar Guerini's limited lifetime warranty and free Pit Stop tune-up program—now that's what we call value added!

FRANCHI RENAISSANCE SPORTING

This mid-priced Renaissance Sporting from Italian maker Franchi came with top-end features like an adjustable comb, extended choke tubes, and ported and mid-vent barrels.

FRANCHI RAPTOR 712

Franchi's Raptor 712 semi-auto shotgun was designed to be durable gun without sacrificing looks. The upgraded Turkish walnut stock received the WeatherCoat process that impregnated the wood and allowed it to shed water in a downpour.

FRANCHI I-12 SPORTING

All eyes will be on you to see if your skills match the beauty of the wood and lines on Franchi's 1-12 Sporting. This lightning fast semi-auto with a 30-inch barrel is a force to be reckoned with on the sporting clays field.

REMINGTON VERSA MAX

Remington's Versa Max may rival its ancestral 1100 model for numbers sold. The Big Green seems to churn out this insanely popular semi-auto in a new configuration every day. To wit, the lineup now includes an all-synthetic pick, while camo lovers get a Mossy Oak Duck Blind and Realtree AP versions. All come with soft rubber overmolds in grip places, adjustable cheekpieces, Remington's super-thick SuperCell recoil pad, and length-of-pull shim spacer kits.

SMITH & WESSON ELITE GOLD

Smith & Wesson experimented with a line of finely crafted double-barrel shotguns for a short time. Included in the line up was a straight-grip, low-profile side-by-side called the Elite Gold. It was available in 20-gauge, with either 26- or 28-inch barrels. On the over/under side of things was the Elite Silver shotgun with a beautiful case colored receiver. The gun wore 30-inch tubes, making it a great choice for both sporting clays competitors and pheasant hunters.

BENELLI CORDOBA

If you know anything about shooting doves in the country of Argentina, then you know it's a high-volume affair—as in thousands of birds falling to the pellets emerging from your gun. Benelli designed its synthetic-stocked Cordoba semi-auto 12- and 20-gauge shotguns with just that kind of case after case shooting in mind, employing a slickly angled stock for fast handling. It also employes Benelli's ComforTech system, which reduces barrel climb by as much as 69 percent over similar semi-autos—and when the doves fly as fast and furious as they do south of the border, that's one feature you and your shoulder will appreciate most of all.

BENELLI SUPER VINCI

It doesn't get much easier to maintain than the Super Vinci shotgun from Benelli, which breaks down into just three modular pieces. There's the QuadraFit buttstock with a simple turn-and-lock attachment to the receiver, the Trigger Group/Forearm module, and the Barrel/Receiver section. Simple, reliable, durable. The gun is available in black synthetic or camoed in Realtree APG or MAX4.

BENELLI SPORT II

The ComfortTech recoil system in Benelli's beautifully walnut-stocked Sport II semi-auto lets competitive clay shooters stay in the game round after round after round. One of the fastest-cycling guns around, this shotgun also patterns densely for definitive "Xs" on the score-card, and its super-cool looks sure stand it apart from all those over/unders on the stage rack.

UGB25 Xcel

Patented

UGB25 Xcel   BERETTA

BERETTA UGB25 XCEL

Competitive trap shooters can be an uptight bunch. When on the line, they like it quieter than the 18th hole at Augusta, will call for a reshoot if the wind behaves like, well, wind, and more than a few scream bloody murder if the empty hull from a just-fired semi-auto ejects near them (the nerve!). All stereo-typing and kidding aside, semi-autos can pose a problem for range officers and shooters alike, as unlike an over/under or break-open single-shot, it's so often hard to tell when one is unloaded and safe. Beretta fixed that with its break-open semi-auto UGB25 Xcel. The ingenious single-barrel design provides the same point of impact shot-to-shot, while Beretta's totally unique locking system actually allows the gun to break open for empty-safe viewing.

BERETTA A400 X-CEL SPORTING

Benchrest shooters are the shooters most notorious for being picky about their ammunition, but there are also shotgunners out there who rival their level of tweakiness. For those scattergun lovers who can't stop fooling with a tenth of a grain of powder here and there, Beretta offers up its A400 Xcel Sporting. The turquoise receiver houses Beretta's revolutionary GunPod system that digitally reads out ambient air temperature, cartridge pressure, and numbers of rounds fired.

CZ WINGSHOOTER

An eye-catching twist on engraving really brings the CZ Wingshooter to life. A striking contrast of blue, gold, and stainless is both unique and attractive. We especially like that CZ builds this gun in a traditional, non-ejector .410-bore that has fixed chokes in Improved and Modified. For 12-gauge and 20-gauge shooters, the gun chambers 3-inch shells and comes with the American preferred auto-ejectors.

STOEGER P350

You can run any 12-gauge shell you want, from standard 2¾-inch through the magnum 3½-inchers, through Stoeger's P350 pump. The Steady Grip version, complete with full-coverage camo, is made specifically for turkey hunting.

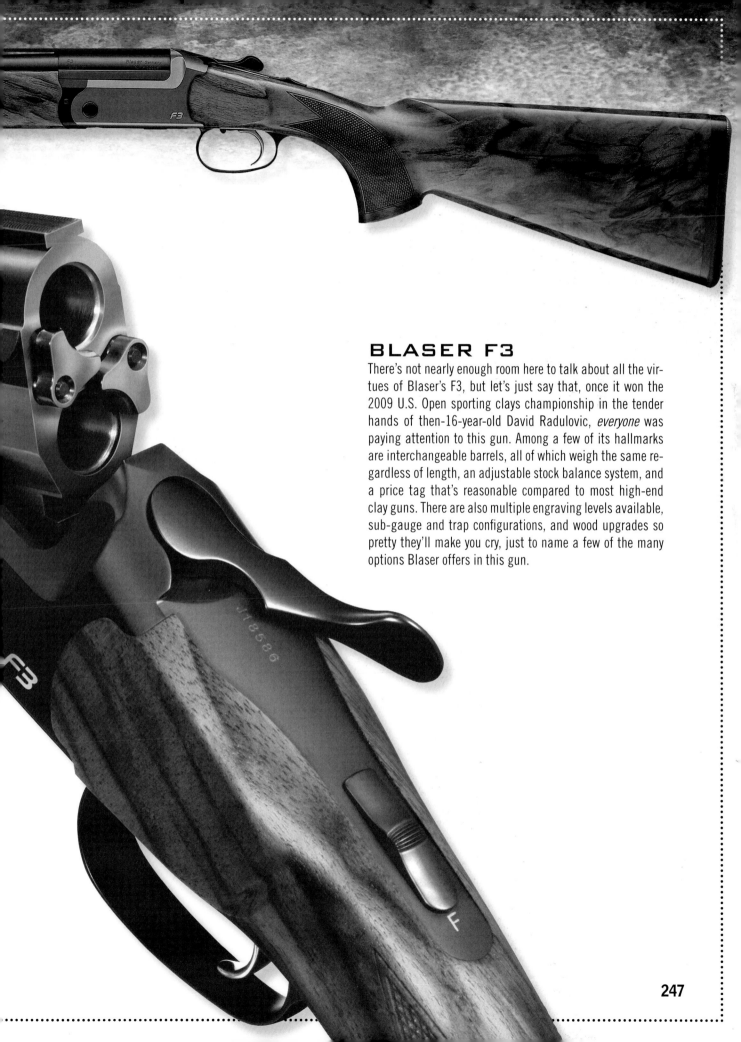

BLASER F3

There's not nearly enough room here to talk about all the virtues of Blaser's F3, but let's just say that, once it won the 2009 U.S. Open sporting clays championship in the tender hands of then-16-year-old David Radulovic, *everyone* was paying attention to this gun. Among a few of its hallmarks are interchangeable barrels, all of which weigh the same regardless of length, an adjustable stock balance system, and a price tag that's reasonable compared to most high-end clay guns. There are also multiple engraving levels available, sub-gauge and trap configurations, and wood upgrades so pretty they'll make you cry, just to name a few of the many options Blaser offers in this gun.

WINCHESTER SXP

A centered balance point adds to the controllability of Winchester's SXP pump shotgun. It comes in a plethora of configurations, including a rugged black synthetic stock model for field use, a short-barreled option for home-defense, and camoed selections for waterfowl hunting. A rifle sighted, rifled barrel slug gun is also an option.

THOMPSON/CENTER ENCORE

Variety is what Thompson/Center is all about. This reputable company also includes single-shot shotguns in its lineup of superior single-shot handguns and bolt-action rifles. Choose the vent rib for turkey hunting or as a wonderfully extra-safe way to introduce new shooters to the clay shooting sports.

WINCHESTER SUPER X3

Winchester has never had a semi-auto shotgun make it big, like its over/under Model 101 did. That may be changing, with the growing popularity of the Super X3. This competition-worthy gun earns itself a nicely figured adjustable stock, a lightweight aluminum receiver, barrel porting, and back-boring in its sporting configuration. All sorts of clay busting fun in this 12-gauge!

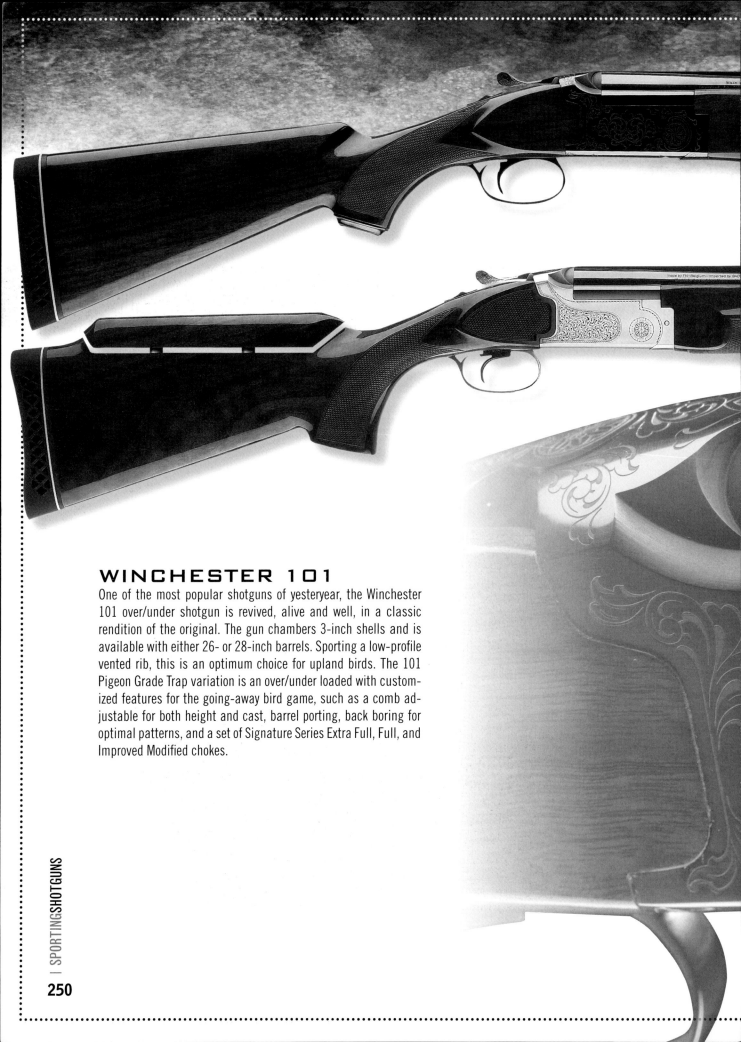

WINCHESTER 101

One of the most popular shotguns of yesteryear, the Winchester 101 over/under shotgun is revived, alive and well, in a classic rendition of the original. The gun chambers 3-inch shells and is available with either 26- or 28-inch barrels. Sporting a low-profile vented rib, this is an optimum choice for upland birds. The 101 Pigeon Grade Trap variation is an over/under loaded with customized features for the going-away bird game, such as a comb adjustable for both height and cast, barrel porting, back boring for optimal patterns, and a set of Signature Series Extra Full, Full, and Improved Modified chokes.

BROWNING 625 GOLDEN CLAYS

One of the most popular guns on the sporting clays circuit is Browning's Citori-based 625 over/under. Clay busters benefit from lengthened forcing cones that improve patterns, barrel porting that dampens muzzle rise, and between-barrel venting that reduces weight on longer barrel sets.

BROWNING UNSINGLE

If trap is your game, then you know point of impact is a big deal when you're working backwards through the handicap yardages. Browning's Unsingle, in both single and double-barrel offerings, has a fully adjustable rib that allows the user to change the gun's point of impact, which should put more "Xs" on the score card.

BROWNING CITORI MAPLE LIGHTNING

This one's certainly an eye-catcher! Browning's traditional Citori Lightning gets a stock makeover in, of all things, maple, a wood that's usually reserved for rifles. Nicely done, all the way around, with tight checkering at the round-knob pistol grip and fore-end, the model is available in a 3-inch 12-gauge with a 26-inch barrel, or as a 3-inch 20-gauge with either 28- or 26-inch barrels available.

BROWNING A-BOLT

Simple, practical, reliable—these are three features you want in any gun, including a slug shotgun. Browning's A-Bolt shotgun, complete with a two-round magazine for a three-round total capacity, employs the company's super-slick A-bolt action for super-fast cycling. Available in a straight hardwood, black synthetic, or Mossy Oak Break-Up Infinity with Dura-Touch Armor Coating.

MERKEL 40E/45E

Side-by-sides have never really caught on in the States, but for those who do appreciate their grace and handleability, you'll want to take a look at the 40E and 45E from German maker Merkel. The 40E goes completely Old World, with a low placed cheek-piece and sling swivel studs, while the 45E is nothing but gorgeousness, with its straight stock, fine checkering, and beautiful engraving. Just can't get into the swing of things with a side-by-side but still want a gun with European influence? Then Merkel's over/under 200 series gives you exactly that.

WEATHERBY PA-08 YOUTH

Weatherby has transitioned through a bevy of shotgun action types and models over the years, so we were especially thrilled to see the company offer a brand new pump-action designed strictly for young shooters. The 3-inch 20-gauge will wear a perfectly shortened 12½-inch length of pull stock and a maneuverable, 22-inch chrome-lined barrel. The works weigh under six pounds and retails under $450.

MOSSBERG 935

Chambering up to 3½-inch 12-gauge shells, the 935 Magnum Turkey from Mossberg comes in both regular and pistol-grip stock variations. Barrels on the semi-automatic shotgun are overbored for optimum patterning, and that's of paramount importance when a trophy longbeard is 50 yards out and won't come closer.

Mossberg JIC

Hunting or backpacking in wet and soggy conditions demands a backup gun that can take it. Mossberg's 500 JIC—Just in Case—Cruiser comes in a waterproof, olive drab carry tube that has a matching survival kit. The Sandstorm version comes in an uber-cool urban camo pattern, while the Mariner comes in a bright orange waterproof case and has both a knife and multi-tool with it.

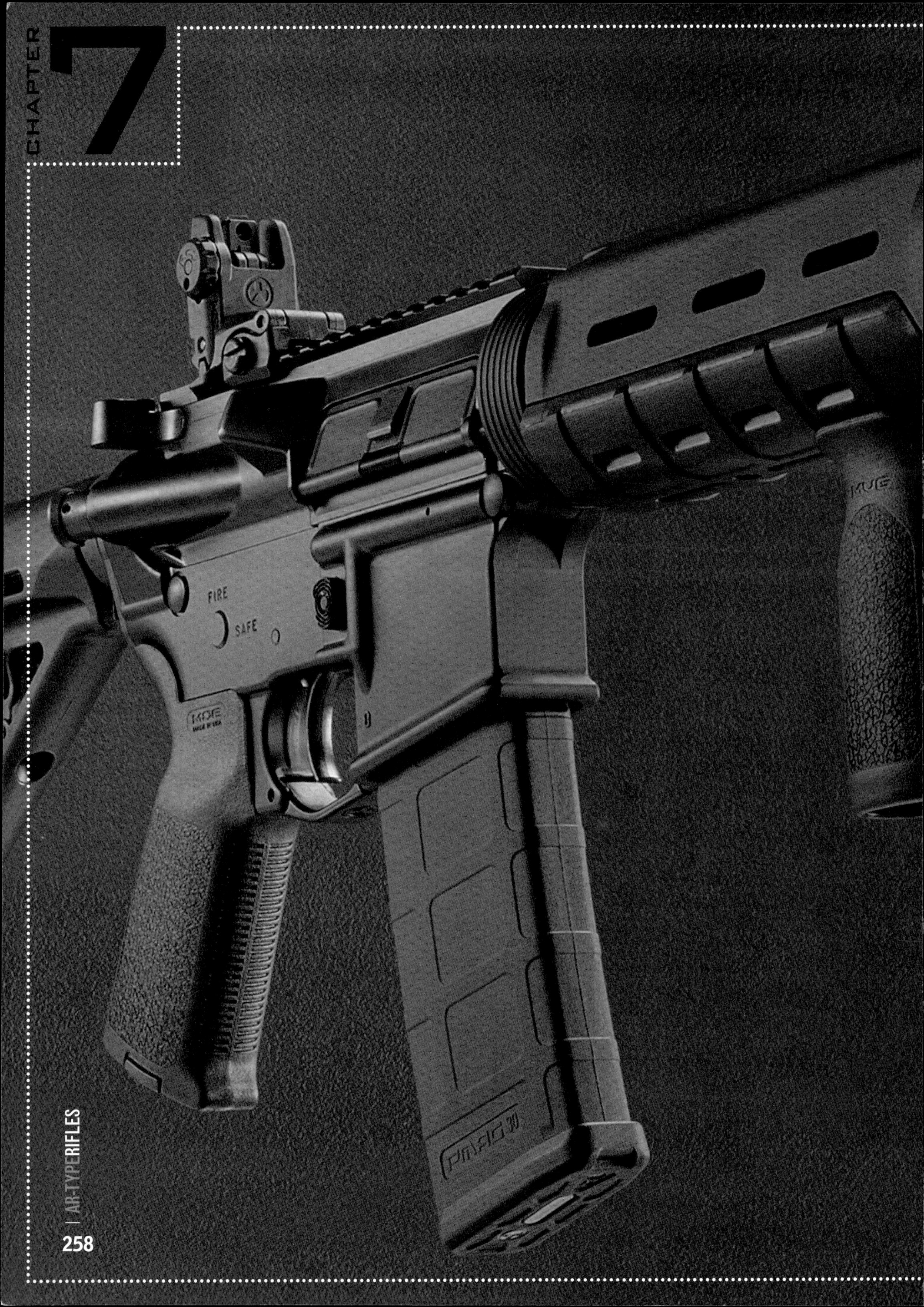
FIRE
SAFE
MOE
PMAG 30

AR-TYPE RIFLES

AR-style rifles continue to be a hot commodity, much as they have for the better part of the last decade. But the action nowadays isn't what it was during the maelstrom of the post-2008 presidential election and the resulting fallout, lovingly referred to as the "Obama effect." Coupled with widespread ammunition shortages during that period, post-election hysteria skyrocketed sales of ARs to heights never before seen, forcing most companies onto months-long backlogs.

Today, in contrast to the AR hoarding of the last few years, gun buyers are calming down and are now seeking rifles designed for more specific uses. The biggest trend is the almost fanatical interest in ARs chambered for 7.62 NATO (.308 Win.). These long-range rapid-fire guns make the ultimate sniper or designated marksman rifle (DMR) and are giving bolt-actions a run for their money. With some manufacturers boasting ½-MOA accuracy, conventional assumptions about accuracy potential in the AR platform are quite literally getting blown to smithereens.

One of the first companies to manufacture a factory-ready AR in this style was Armalite, with its AR-10 SuperSASS (Semi-Automatic Sniper System). This rifle, originally designed for the military and now available in a civilian model, is a semi-automatic optics-ready precision shooter. Like other rifles of its ilk, it has a 20-inch stainless steel match grade barrel and finely tuned National Match trigger. The forged flattop with its Picatinny rail makes mounting a scope a breeze and the quad-railed handguard accepts nearly any bipod/sling combination. Armalite announced at the 2012 SHOT (Shooting, Hunting and Outdoor Trade) Show that both the AR-A10 SuperSASS and AR-A10A4 Carbine would now accept third-party magazines, such as the popular Magpul PMAGS.

Other guns in this category include the LWRCI Rapid Engagement Precision Rifle (REPR), DPMS 308 Recon, Heckler & Koch G28 Marksman, and the Les Baer .308 Semi-Auto Sniper.

AR piston guns—like the Ruger SR-556 and SIG 516—are another craze, as of late. Piston operation, as opposed to direct impingement, reduces heat and keeps carbon out of the chamber and bolt area, improving reliability and accuracy. In fact, today you'll find nearly every one of the AR manufacturers offering at least one gas piston gun in their lineups. Likewise, aftermarket companies have been quick to capitalize on the trend with conversion kits.

One new AR that is bridging the gap between .308 Win. and .223 Rem. is the Colt LE901-16S. Its modular design allows you to change calibers simply by popping a couple pins. The result? You have two rifles in one, aptly handling close-quarters battle and long-range sniping with a simple swap of the upper.

The AR world is replete with new calibers, too. One example is the 6.8mm Remington SPC, which occupies the ballistic territory roughly between .308 and .223. With the average law enforcement sniper engagement reaching a scant 64 yards, the slightly heftier 6.8 could fill a role for police marksmen. Then again, there are comparably chambered ARs—like the Rock River Arms LAR-47—that shoot the Russian 7.62X39mm cartridge and accept AK-47 mags. One of the newest cartridges in .30-caliber is the .300 AAC Blackout (.300 BLK). Developed by Advanced Armament Corp., it's causing quite a stir in the AR community. The idea behind this hot little number is that it doesn't reduce magazine capacity and allows the use of the AR's standard bolt. Bullets in weights of 115- to 125-grain match the ballistics of the 7.62x39mm AK and surpass the 5.56mm. At 300 meters, the 300BLK has 16.7-percent more energy than a 7.62x39mm. Other new calibers gaining notoriety in AR circles include the 6X45, .30 Gremlin, .30 Remington AR, 6.5 Grendal, .458 SOCOM, .22 LR, and even 9mm!

—Corey Graff, Gun Digest Online Content Editor

ROCK RIVER ARMS LAR-15 HUNTER

With its WYL-Ehide camo—which is anodized to the lower, upper, charging handle, trigger guard and hand guard—the Rock River Arms LAR-15 Hunter (above) is the ultimate vermin snuffer. Ideal for the coyote hunter, this attractive AR is a 5.56 NATO (.223 Rem.) rifle with 16-inch barrel, RRA's Tactical Muzzle Break, and standard two-stage trigger. It features Rock River's distinctive half-quad free-float mid-length handguard. The high-quality Hogue grip and RRA Operator CAR Stock make this AR critter-getter look even better.

AR15.COM

AR15.com is the gargantuan Internet forum for all things AR. Now the online superpower is building one of the toughest-looking and most functional AR rifles you'll find (left). The lower was developed with a fully ambidextrous set of controls, enabling complete bilateral operation of the weapon. It is the first production lower to feature a 45-degree selector and, combined with the super-fast Geissele S3G trigger, this means the rifle is capable of extremely quick engagements and follow-up shots. Topped with a simple and reliable piston system, which is also Ion-Bond coated, this rifle can go tens of thousands of rounds without maintenance, making it the ideal platform for duty, competition, or self-defense. Finished with a no-nonsense free float rail and a choice of Magpul furniture, this rifle has everything you need and nothing you don't right out of the box.

ROCK RIVER ARMS LAR-47

All your comrades will want the LAR-47 (above) from Rock River Arms. Chambered in 7.62 X 39mm Russian, this AR-meets-the-AK accepts standard AK mags. The LAR-47 lower and upper are proprietary, though most of the other features are standard AR, including the two-stage trigger group, 16-inch barrel, A2 flash suppressor, ambidextrous magazine release and RRA's six-position tactical CAR Stock.

ROCK RIVER ARMS LAR-15 PRO SERIES ELITE

There isn't much customization needed on the Rock River Arms LAR-15 Pro Series Elite (below). Representative of many of the higher-end ARs on the market, it is chambered for 5.56 NATO (.223 Rem.). One of the first things you notice about it is its distinctive RRA muzzle break. The rifle sports RRA's ERGO Grip and Operator CAR Stock. It operates on a mid-length gas system, and the barrel is 16 inches. The Elite Operator has a two-stage trigger and what the company calls its Winter Trigger Guard, giving you additional room to fit those extra-thick glove-protected fingers into the trigger area. The package comes with a Surefire M910A-WH Weapon Light and an EOTech XPS2-0 HWS Sight.

LWRCI IC

LWRCI's Individual Carbine (IC) was developed for, appropriately, the U.S. Army's Individual Carbine program. It is based on the standard M4/AR-15 spec, but with some radical improvements. It features a fully ambidextrous lower receiver and dual controls for the bolt catch and release, mag release, and fire control, allowing the user to easily transition to their offhand side in the event of an injury or when encountering barriers that inhibit conventional firing positions. The upper is distinctive looking and represents the evolution of the company's M6A2-SPR (Special Purpose Rifle) platform. The two-position gas block is user-configurable for Normal or Suppressed fire. The full-size IC has a 14.7-inch barrel and is covered in a non-infrared-reflective Cerakote Stealth covering.

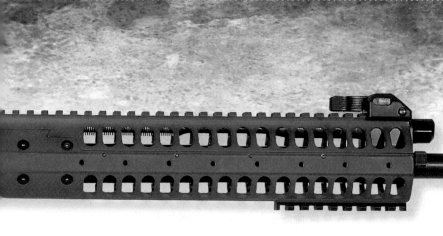

LWRCI REPR

Nothing invokes images of the gaunt, hooded specter with his scythe like a .308 semi-auto sniper named the "REPR." The letters stand for Rapid Engagement Precision Rifle, and it's LWRCI's answer to the AR-platform sniper rifle, also known as a designated marksman rifle (DMR). Its ability to put multiple rounds of devastating 7.62 NATO (.308) on target accurately and then switch to a 12-inch upper in seconds for close-in battle, makes it an ideal weapon for a variety of combat roles. It comes in four models: the Standard (12.7- and 16.1-inch barrels); Designated Marksman Rifle (18-inch); and Sniper (20-inch) configurations. New for 2012, LWRCI is offering a 16-inch version with a fluted barrel to shave weight and reduce longitudinal stresses that can contribute to "stringing."

ARMALITE AR-10A4

This hard-hitting carbine from Armalite, chambered in 7.62 NATO (.308 Win.), is compact and powerful with a 16-inch barrel and collapsible buttstock. The AR-10A4 features a clamping gas block, which allows the removable front sight to be rotated to zero. This assures that the rear sight is centered, giving full left and right windage movement when shooting in strong winds. As part of Armalite's "A" family of rifles, this new offering also accepts third-party mags from Magpul (PMAGS), Knight's Armament, and DPMS, in addition to the traditional style "waffle" mags.

ARMALITE AR-10A SUPERSASS

Armalite's AR10A SuperSASS is a suppressor-ready 7.62 rifle that can now accept third-party mags from Magpul (PMAGS), Knight's Armament, and DPMS. It has an adjustable gas system to fine-tune performance with a variety of ammunition and suppressors. Its 20-inch stainless steel match grade barrel and two-stage match trigger group—first stage 2½ pounds, second stage 4½ to 5 pounds—ensure pinpoint accuracy. With a quad Picatinny rail handguard and adjustable Magpul buttstock, it is highly customizable. The rifle weights 11.84 pounds and shoots 1 MOA from the factory.

DPMS 300 BLACKOUT

Chambered for the awesome .300 AAC Blackout (BLK) cartridge—the hot .30-caliber number with ballistics on par with the Russian 7.62x39mm—the DPMS 300 Blackout comes with the company's innovative M111 free-float tube, allowing you to choose how much rail you want for accessories or grip. The rifle has a 4150 chrome-lined barrel in a heavy contour. This AR is equipped with either an AAC Blackout Suppressor Adapter or an inert mock suppressor for looks.

DPMS 308 RECON

Bridging the gap between the carbine and rifle is the new DPMS 308 Recon. As the name implies, this AR-style gun is chambered in .308. It packs sub-MOA accuracy in a compact, versatile tactical carbine, making it ideal for tactical applications, competition, or even hog hunting. The Recon features a 16-inch mid-length, stainless Hbar 1:10 twist barrel; a four-rail free-float handguard; Magpul MOE stock and Grip; Gen2 Back Up sights; and an AAC Blackout suppressor adapter.

LES BAER
POLICE SPECIAL

Chambered in either .223 or 6X45, the Police Special from custom builder Les Baer is all business. This 16-inch AR was designed to include every important feature a police officer wants and none of the stuff he doesn't. The newest version of this carbine includes a new LBC national match carrier, a new collapsible stock/pistol grip package, and a very special LBC flip-up front sight. As a patrol carbine, the Les Baer Police Special is intentionally devoid of the amateur add-ons that cheapen the purpose and limit the usefulness of a police rifle for real street work. Les guarantees these rugged and simple rifles will shoot 1 MOA out of the box.

LES BAER .308
SEMI-AUTO SNIPER

Machined from a milled billet of 7075-T6-51 aluminum, the Les Baer .308 Semi-Auto Sniper is classic Les—custom made and hand built. Les Baer's obsession with quality and attention to detail are immediately apparent, due in large part to the LBC benchrest 416R stainless steel barrel with cut rifling, a feature that has become a hallmark of all Les Baer custom rifles. This .308-caliber rifle is available with either an 18- or 20-inch barrel and the Enforcer muzzle break, which dampens recoil to the level of a .223. The Geissele two-stage trigger group promotes accuracy, which Les guarantees to be ½-MOA from the factory.

HECKLER & KOCH G28

The G28 pictured above, from German powerhouse Heckler & Koch, is the new designated marksman rifle for the German army. Available in Standard Configuration and Patrol Configuration (3½ pounds/1.6 kilograms lighter with a shorter handguard and less powerful 1-8X scope), both G28 variants come standard with adjustable buttstocks. The G28 features a special low observable-infrared green/brown (RAL8000) color finish. H&K's standard complete weapons system configuration features Schmidt & Bender telescopic sights (3-20X50 or 1-8X24), red dot sight (Aimpoint Micro T1), a laser light module (Rheinmetall Soldier Electronics LLM01-RAL8000), night sight (Qioptiq MERLIN LR), a thermal sight (Insight CNVD-T35), and laser rangefinders (Jenoptik HLR15 or Vectronix PLRF15).

HECKLER & KOCH MR556A1

Heckler & Koch's MR556A1, below, is the civilian version of the MK416 used by the military (and recently adopted by the United States Marine Corps). The MR556A1 uses the H&K proprietary gas piston operating system, employing a piston and a solid operating "pusher" rod in place of the gas tube normally found in AR15/M16/M4-style firearms. The result is less fouling in the chamber area and greater shot-to-shot accuracy. The H&K Free Floating Rail System (FFRS) handguard has four MIL-STD-1913 Picatinny rails and allows all current accessories, sights, lights, and aimers used on M4/M16-type arms to be fitted to the MR Series. The un-chromed barrel—chambered in 5.56 NATO (.223) has an internal profile of six lands and grooves with a 1:7 twist. The thick, heavy-contour 16½-inch MR556A1 barrel contributes to its accuracy.

SMITH & WESSON M&P15 300 WHISPER

Not your grandpappy's deer rifle, the M&P15 300 Whisper is designed to shoot either the .300 Whisper or .300 AAC Blackout. These .30-caliber cartridges are devastating deep-woods deer getters. The round is known for its low recoil and soft muzzle blast, making follow-up shots a breeze. The 1:7½ twist barrel is compatible with a variety of ammunition choices from 110- to 220-plus-grain loads. This distinctive-looking sporting rifle is finished in Realtree APG camo. Its flattop rail will accept any optics you need, including that 4X scope that's been itching for a ride on a new deer rifle.

SMITH & WESSON M&P15 VTAC II

Featuring Smith & Wesson's Mid-Length System—designed to reduce recoil and promote faster follow-up shots—the M&P15 VTAC II came about as a team effort between S&W, Kyle Lamb, and Viking Tactics. Internal attention to detail is evident in its 16-inch barrel, which has 5R rifling to reduce copper fouling. The barrel is outfitted with S&W's patented Enhanced Flash Hider. The VTAC/TROY 13-inch Extreme TRX Handguard has two, two-inch adjustable Picatinny-style rails. Shooters will appreciate this handguard's ability to reduce heat transfer.

SMITH & WESSON M&P15 MOE MID

A collaboration between Magpul and Smith & Wesson, the M&P15 MOE Mid is available in black and flat dark earth finishes. The lower is stamped Magpul. The AR features what's called the Mid-Length System, which results in lower recoil and better accuracy for increased second shot hit probability, and the magwell on this .223-chambered AR is flared for extra-fast mag changes. The handguard is Magpul's, with the MVP Vertical Grip standard, and the MBUS rear sight and included PMAGS all Magpul as well. The rifle even comes with Magpul Dynamic's *The Art of the Tactical Carbine Volumes I & II* DVD set.

SIG M400

SIG Sauer's M400 is a true AR platform based on the direct impingement gas-operated system. With an overall length of 36.6 inches (32.5 with the stock collapsed), this 5.56 NATO (.223) is a handy AR for the tactical professional, hunter, or competitive shooter. The attractive OD Green version is distinctive and comes with Magpul handguard, stock, and grip. The 1:7 twist chrome-lined 16-inch barrel is topped off with an M16 A2-type flash suppressor.

SIG516
PATROL FDE

The SIG516 Patrol FDE (Flat Dark Earth) from SIG Sauer is similar to SIG's M400 carbine, with one exception—this model is a piston-operated gun. The SIG short-stroke gas pushrod operating system reduces chamber debris and allows the rifle to run cleaner and cooler. This system, along with the SIG Sauer fully supported proprietary extractor, enables the SIG516 to be one of the only rifles to pass NATO's "Over the Beach" test. A 16-inch chrome-lined barrel is chambered in 5.56mm NATO and is surrounded by a free-floating M1913 quad rail. The top rail is optic-ready and includes the SIG Sauer flip-up iron sights.

SIG716

Chambered for the 7.62 NATO (.308) cartridge, the SIG716 is the big brother to the 516. Like its smaller cousin, this rifle uses the short-stroke piston operating system with a four-position adjustable gas valve to keep debris out of the chamber area. An ideal designated marksman rifle (DMR), the SIG716's overall length reaches 37.4 inches and the rifle weighs 9.3 pounds. It comes with Magpul PMAGS and a removable flip-up rear sight. Naturally, the Picatinny-style flattop rail is the perfect surface for the addition of a scope.

COLT LE6920MP-B

The Colt LE6920MP-B draws on the combat experience of its close relative, the Colt M4. The carbine has a 16.1-inch chrome-lined barrel, with a 1:7 twist to choke down a variety of ammunition with no trouble at all. Teaming up with Magpul, Colt's added many of the most popular aftermarket accessories, including MOE handguard, carbine stock, pistol grip, and vertical grip. The flat-top receiver comes standard with Magpul's backup sight. The .223-chambered carbine is a direct gas system gun with locking bolt and comes in matte black.

COLT LE901-16S

The Colt LE901-16S is a select-fire rifle designed to allow you to change the upper from 5.56 to 7.62 in a matter of seconds. The Colt LE901-16S rifle weighs only 9.4 pounds and measures 37.5 inches with the stock extended. It has an effective range of 700 meters and a rate of fire between 700 and 950 rounds per minute when configured for .308. Exceptional accuracy comes by way of the free-floated, 16-inch, chrome-lined barrel and one-piece monolithic upper receiver. All operating controls on the LE901-16S are ambidextrous, including the magazine release, bolt catch, and fire control selector. The monolithic rail covers the fore-end and is suitable for mounting optics. The back up iron sight (BUIS) is standard on the rifle.

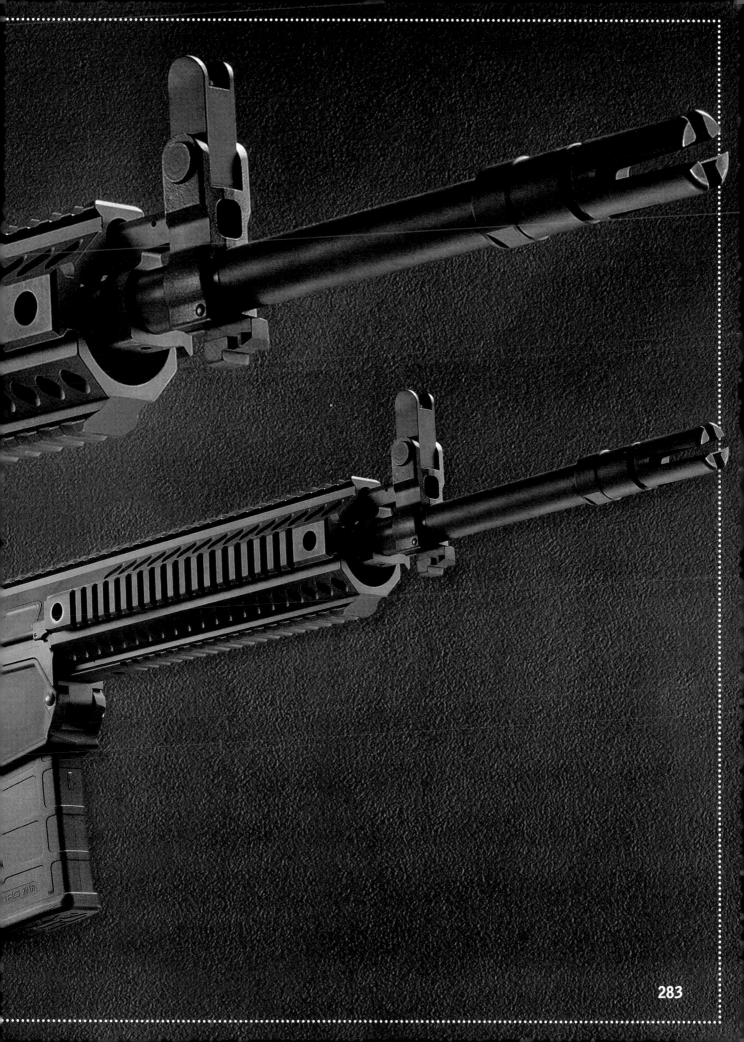

RUGER SR-556

Ruger is one of the newest companies to offer a piston AR. The SR-556's two-stage piston driven operating system features a fully adjustable gas regulator. All the by-products of the gas system are vented out the bottom of the gas block, keeping contaminants free of the bolt carrier. Ruger says this improves reliability and accuracy. The SR-556 also comes with distinctive Troy Industries rail covers and folding Battle Sights front and rear. This 5.56 NATO (.223) AR accepts and ships with Magpul PMAGS standard.

RUGER SR-22

The Ruger SR-22 is an autoloading rimfire rifle based on the AR platform. In fact, the gun is built with the same ergonomics as Ruger's SR-556, except it uses the Ruger 10/22 action. The flattop receiver is ideally made for any optics you might want to add, and, given the affordability of .22 rimfire ammunition, the entire concept makes for a genuinely useful training gun, if not also a super-fun plinker or small-game rifle.

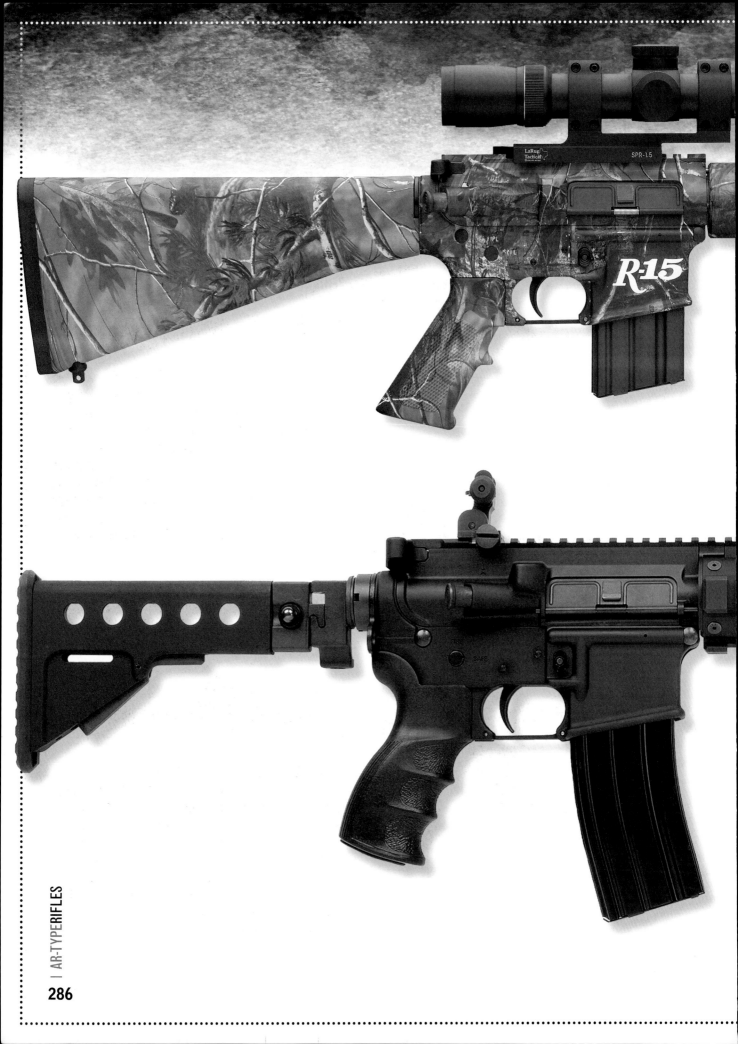

REMINGTON R-15 VTR

The new R-15 VTR modular repeating rifle by Remington was designed for the modern varmint hunter. Chambered in .223, its free-floated button-rifled ChroMoly barrel has a recessed hunting crown for superior accuracy—truly bad news for any coyote or fox. In addition, Remington designed a new single-stage trigger for this gun that has nothing but accuracy in mind. The camo treatment is Advantage MAX-1 HD in full coverage on the stock, receiver, grip, and handguard. The R-15 accepts most aftermarket mags.

PARA USA TTR

We dig it! Para USA's TTR (Target Tactical Rifle) puts you back on target faster after each shot with its Delayed Impingement Gas System (DIGS) to help you win your next match. Para claims no other AR platform will recover shot-to-shot as fast as this one, thanks to the recoil system being positioned over the barrel, where it works to push the barrel back onto the target, instead of allowing recoil to force the entire gun back into the shooter's shoulder and the barrel up in the air.

DPMS ARCTIC PANTHER

You can shoot just about anything you want to with the Arctic Panther from DPMS, but this white-garbed AR is a particularly sweet choice for winter coyotes. Clad in a hard coat anodized Mil Spec white on the A3 flattop receiver and fore-end, this .223 has a 20-inch fluted and Teflon-coated barrel. An optics-only rifle (i.e., DPMS did away with the iron sights you wouldn't use anyway), it weighs a totally tote-able nine pounds when empty.

DMPS PANTHER 6.5 CREEDMOOR

Hi-power match rifles shooting .223 and .308 are a dime a dozen. Be different and shoot a DPMS Panther 6.5 Creedmoor! Introduced by Hornady, in 2007, the cartridge mimics the .300 Win. Mag.'s flight, but with less recoil and a high ballistic co-efficient, both of which can be a huge bonus in long, drawn-out matches.

DPMS AGENCY

DPMS says its Agency tac carbine is a full-boat package just chock full of upgrades, including an ERGO ambi-grip, DPMS Pardus carbine stock, and two-stage trigger. Oh, and let there be light! DPMS ditched the removable carry handle and slapped on not only a Magonel flip-up rear sight, but also an EoTech 512 Holosight and a SureFire M73 handguard with an attached SureFire M951XM weapon's light.

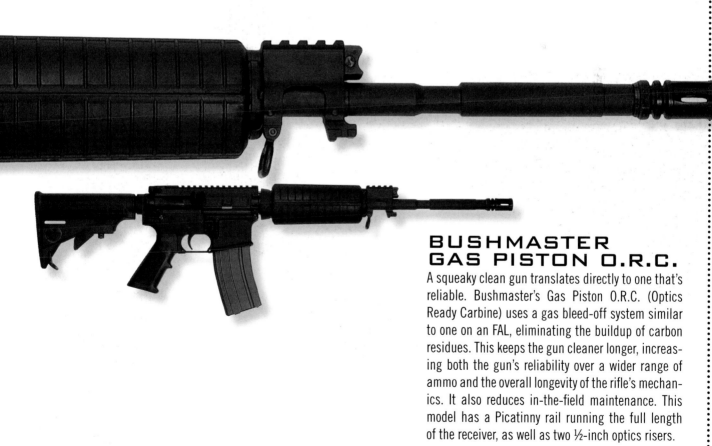

BUSHMASTER GAS PISTON O.R.C.

A squeaky clean gun translates directly to one that's reliable. Bushmaster's Gas Piston O.R.C. (Optics Ready Carbine) uses a gas bleed-off system similar to one on an FAL, eliminating the buildup of carbon residues. This keeps the gun cleaner longer, increasing both the gun's reliability over a wider range of ammo and the overall longevity of the rifle's mechanics. It also reduces in-the-field maintenance. This model has a Picatinny rail running the full length of the receiver, as well as two ½-inch optics risers.

BUSHMASTER UIR

Straight from Bushmaster's Custom Shop comes the company's UIR, or Urban Interdiction Rifle. Designed with portability first in mind, the 16½-inch match-barreled rifle is just 34½ inches overall with the stock collapsed. It wears a bevy of Magpul and Midwest Industries upgrades, including the Magpul MIAD pistol grip and enhanced trigger guard, and Midwest's mid-length free-floating handguard.

BUSHMASTER PMR

If you want perfect score cards in high-power match competition, then Bushmaster's Custom Shop PMR—Precision Marksmen Rifle—is a good place to start. The company designed this one for ink-dot accuracy at 800 yards, even when suppressed, and guarantees sub-MOA out to 300. Lots of premium upgrades on this one, including a Magpul PRS stock and MIAD pistol grip, a hand-lapped stainless match barrel, Geissele DMR trigger, and a SureFire muzzle brake, to name just a few. In .223, naturally, and complete with a limited lifetime warranty—and that's putting some faith in its guns.

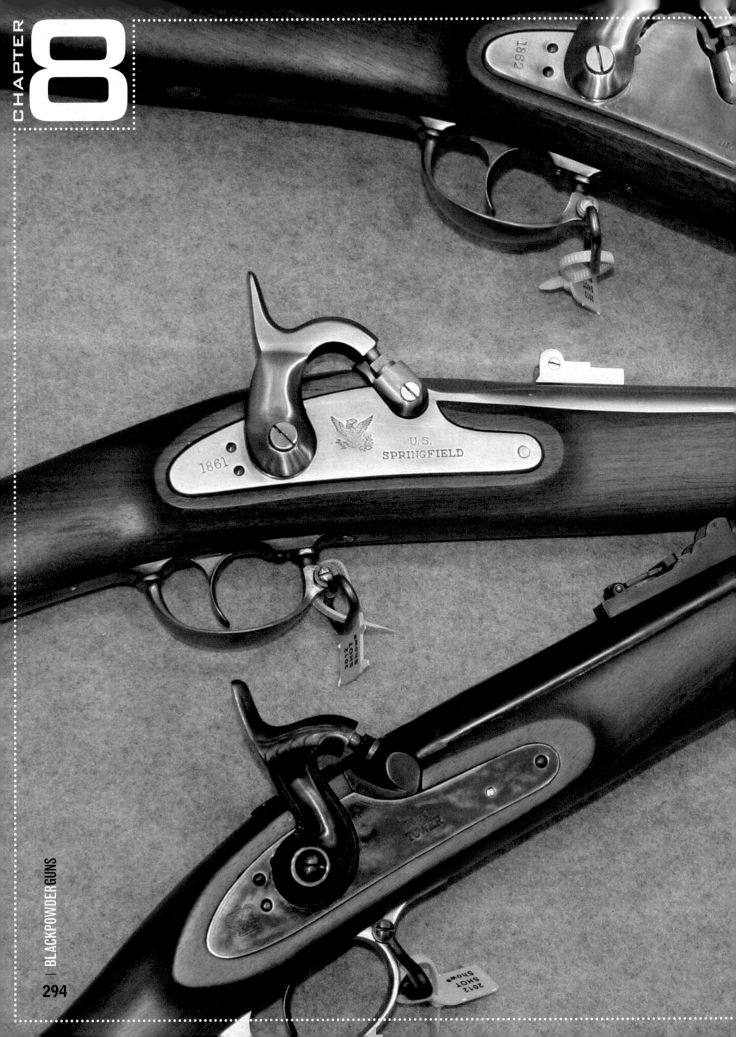

CHAPTER 8

BLACK-POWDER GUNS

Hunting with a blackpowder rifle says something about the person behind the gun. To some it's a closer bonding with nature, while for others it's a greater challenge to their hunting and shooting abilities. Some find it's a way to have a longer or earlier hunting season, and then there are those shooters who simply love the traditional front-loading guns, not only for hunting, but to use in competition events and reenactments of historical battles.

When Tony Knight, founder and former owner of Knight Rifles, introduced his MK-85 inline muzzleloader, in 1985, many people in the industry didn't know what to think. And they certainly didn't see what was coming. Very soon, other inline rifle makers were up and running and, within a few years, big-name firearms manufacturers like Remington and Savage were in the game. For a variety of reasons, the Remington and Savage models are no longer in production, but companies like Knight, Thompson/Center, Traditions, CVA, and many others are offering an enormous choice of blackpowder products, including traditionally styled muzzleloaders. What follows is a look at some of the latest to the scene.

—*Jerry Lee, Editor at Large, Gun Digest Books*

KNIGHT RIFLES MOUNTAINEER

Under new owners, Knight Rifles is alive and well and has relocated from Iowa, to Tennessee. Due to popular demand, the Mountaineer model is now available in .45-caliber, as well as .50 and .52. Options include a straight or thumb-hole stock in several different patterns and colors. Knight Rifles are 100-percent American made. Features of the Mountaineer are a Green Mountain 27-inch free-floated barrel, fully adjustable fiber-optic sights, an adjustable match-grade trigger, and Knight's exclusive Full Plastic Jacket ignition system. Ice or snow, searing heat or freezing cold, no matter what the weather conditions, it'll go bang. The Knight accuracy guarantee lives on, as well, meaning you can expect consistent four-inch groups at 200 yards with your developed loads.

KNIGHT RIFLES LONG RANGE HUNTER

This is one of those rifles that turns heads wherever it's seen. The Long Range Hunter has a striking thumb-hole laminate custom stock with a palm swell, wide beavertail fore-end, and a high comb for comfortable shooting in the field or on the bench. The stock also is a cast-off design and has a HIVIZ recoil pad and sling swivel studs. Twist rate for the 27-inch Green Mountain barrel is 1:28 for .50-caliber, 1:26 for .52. Fully adjustable fiber optic sights and trigger are other custom touches. Ignition is via a shotshell No. 209 primer in a full plastic jacket, or a Western No. 11 and musket cap.

THOMPSON/CENTER
PRO HUNTER FX

The interchangeable barrel models of T/C rifles and handguns have been around for years and really put the company on the map. Not everyone needs this feature, though, so recently T/C began offering a fixed-barrel variation of the Pro Hunter, with the action, stock, and accessories that are available for the Encore Pro Hunter. Our photo shows the Pro Hunter FX with Realtree AP camo stock. You can also get the rifle with a composite stock.

THOMPSON/CENTER
TRIUMPH BONE COLLECTOR

If you watch hunting shows on TV, you probably know Michael Waddell and his *Bone Collector* series on Outdoor Channel. Michael helped T/C design the Bone Collector rifle. It has all the features of the Triumph Magnum Muzzleloader family, with the addition of a Flex Tech stock and a premium fluted barrel. You have a choice of a dark gray composite stock or Realtree's AP camo coverage.

CVA ACCURA

The company slogan is "America's No. 1 Muzzleloader," and CVA bases this claim on sales numbers that beat any other muzzle-loader company. The newest addition to the CVA lineup is the Accura Mountain Rifle, a lighter version of the other Accura break-open models. It's a handy 6.35-pound .50-caliber, with a stainless steel 25-inch fluted barrel and an overall length of 40 inches. CVA's Pro Staff is a group of some of the country's top muzzleloader hunters, and the Accura is a result of their input. It's designed for tough weather conditions, with CVA's own WeatherGuard exterior coating. Other features include the company's patent-pending Quick Release Breech Plug, adjustable trigger, fiber optic sights (or scope mount), and a standard or thumb-hole composite camo stock.

(PHOTO BY WM. HOVEY SMITH.)

TRADITIONS
PURSUIT ULTRALIGHT

Traditions calls its Pursuit Ultralight the lightest muzzleloader in the world. Weight of this break-open .50-caliber is listed at 5.15 pounds. It has a 26-inch Chromoly tapered and fluted barrel and Traditions' exclusive LT-1 alloy frame. The camo pattern is Mossy Oak's Infinity, and the metal finish is a Premium CeraKote. A Quick Relief recoil pad and sling swivel studs are standard features of the stock. A thumbhole version is also available. It's worth mentioning that, as Traditions continues to make advancements with its break-open models, and while other manufacturers are cutting back or eliminating side-hammer flint and percussion rifles, this company, as the name implies, continues to produce a full line of traditional muzzleloaders.

TRADITIONS
VORTEK ULTRALIGHT LDR

Traditions exec Jason Rhodes holding the Vortek Ultralight .50-caliber at the January 2012 SHOT Show, in Las Vegas. It's the only 30-inch barrel break-open muzzleloader on the market. Specifically designed for the long-range shooter, it comes with a 4-12X40mm scope mounted and bore sighted. The stock and fore-end are covered with Reaper Buck Camo, and the alloy frame and barrel are treated with a Premium CeraKote finish. Other features include a drop-out trigger factory set at four pounds, Hogue Comfort-Grip Overmolding, a Quick Relief recoil pad, and Traditions Dual Safety system.

PEDERSOLI CIVIL WAR RIFLES

The Pedersoli company markets replica blackpowder rifles under its own name. Newest to the company's lineup are several rifles commemorating the American Civil War. Shown from the top are a CSA Richmond Rifle, a Springfield, and an Enfield. The Davide Pedersoli company is one of several, fine Italian gunmakers located in Gardone Val Trompia that provide many of the products for Cimarron Firearms.

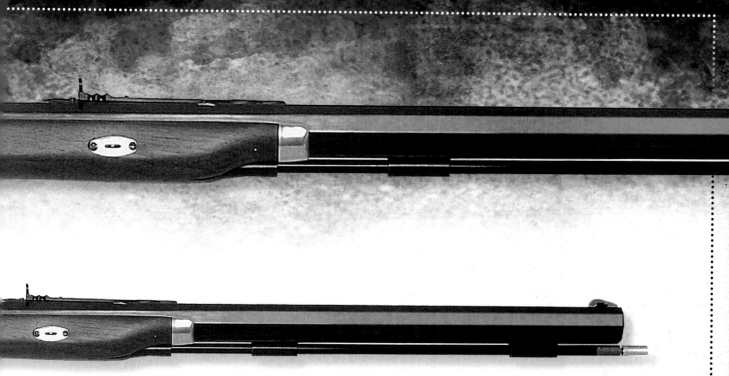

CIMARRON FIREARMS
GIMMER SHARPS HYBRID

For more than a quarter-century, this company has nurtured the Spirit of the West with a wide range of reproductions of Colt's, Winchester, Spencer, Remington, Sharp, and other rifles, handguns, and shotguns. It's always a pleasure to drop by the Cimarron booth at the SHOT Show and look at the latest guns and accessories, many of them made specifically for cowboy action shooting. Among the most interesting recent creations of Cimarron owner Mike Harvey is the Gimmer Sharps Hybrid. By using a No. 209 shotshell primer in a new breech plug, a conventional Sharps rifle is turned into a muzzleloader—and you don't have to use paper cartridges or reload .50-caliber cases. The Hybrid is just like a Gimmer Sharps, with a double-set trigger, side hammer, and 32-inch octagon barrel, but it loads from the muzzle.

CIMARRON FIREARMS
SANTA FE HAWKEN

This new Cimarron model is made by Pedersoli. It has a handsome stock of fancy maple and a shallow-groove, fast-twist, Sharps-style octagon barrel with a length of 30 inches. The .50-caliber Hawken has a case hardened lock and rust brown finish on the barrel and other metal parts. Weight is about 9½ pounds, just right for a steady hold on those long shots.

AIRGUNS

While still a niche group, one of the fastest-growing segments in shooting these days is the airgun category. Not many years ago, it was estimated there were between 25,000 and 50,000 active airgunners in the USA. Estimates today are in the hundreds of thousands, and, according to some sources, as many as five million firearms users plan to include airguns in their future shooting activities.

There are a lot of reasons for the growing popularity of airguns in today's world. Urban sprawl continues around many of our larger towns and cities, making it more and more difficult to find a place to shoot regular firearms. Airguns are quieter and safer, too, and BBs and pellets aren't as fast and don't carry as far as bullets, facts that make their use more neighbor-friendly, in many areas. It must be remembered, however, that airguns are not toys and can cause serious injury and even be fatal.

For generations, airguns have played an important role in teaching the basics of shooting. The classic Daisy Red Ryder lever-action, as well as moderately priced models from other manufacturers, continue to be ideal first guns for youngsters. For more advanced training, some of today's precision pellet guns have excellent triggers and sighting systems. They are capable of serious accuracy and offer an economical way to learn the disciplines of serious shooting.

Another reason for the growth of airguns in recent years is that, generally speaking, there are less restrictive regulations on ownership and transfer. They can be purchased on the Internet and, in most areas, be shipped directly to the buyer. Be sure to know your local laws, however. Some states apply the same laws to airguns as they do to firearms, and there are sometimes age limits, permit requirements, and other restrictions.

The biggest growth area in airgunning is for hunting. This isn't limited to typical airgun targets like rodents or small birds. Serious hunters of small game such as squirrels and rabbits, and game birds such as grouse, quail, and even turkeys, are using airguns, where allowed. And more and more hunters are taking to the field with airguns for bigger game. The more powerful .25- and .357-caliber airgun rifles are capable of taking wild boar and deer at close ranges. There is now even a .50-caliber airgun! Regulations on hunting with airguns vary considerably from state to state so, again, so be sure you know what's permitted in your area.

As this book goes to print, this is a summer Olympics year, and some of the shooting events in London are conducted with airguns. The Olympic games often serve to pique the public's interest in competitive shooting. There are many NRA-sanctioned airgun events held around the country, as well as other less formal competitions at the local level. For information on events in your area, call the National Rifle Association at 703-267-1475, go on line to www.nrahq.org/compete/airgun, or e-mail rifle@nrahq.org.

Airguns generally fall into three basic types: spring piston, pneumatic, and CO_2. The spring-piston type requires the compression of the mainspring to be cocked manually. This pressure is released when the trigger is pulled and the pellet or BB is propelled out of the barrel. The cocking mechanisms are the under-lever, the side-lever, and the break-open.

Pneumatic guns also use a manual cocking system, in this case a pumping motion, usually with the fore-end part of the stock under the barrel. Some require several motions to compress enough air to power the gun, while others only require a single pumping action. The single-pump rifles tend to have the most consistent power and velocity. Very popular today is the PCP (pre-charged pneumatic) design, in which a high-pressure charge of compressed air is contained in a tube, usually located under the barrel. The tube can be charged with either a scuba air tank or a hand pump that usually comes with the rifle.

CO_2 guns get their power from carbon dioxide gas that is stored in a cylinder. The cylinders have to be replaced periodically, as the gas supply decreases. CO_2-powered guns are generally not as powerful as the other types, but are more convenient for multiple shots.

There were more than 20 different airgun manufacturers displaying their wares at the 2012 Shooting, Hunting and Outdoor Trade (SHOT) Show in Las Vegas. What follows are some of the models that caught our eye.

—Jerry Lee, Editor at Large, Gun Digest Books

FX GLADIATOR MKII

The Gladiator MKII above is the newest model from the Swedish company FX Airguns and is an improved version of the Verminator MK2, with the addition of a front air cylinder having three different power settings. The cocking system is the side-lever type, and among this airgun's other features are a match-grade trigger, multi-shot magazine, pressure gauge, and fully adjustable stock. The Gladiator is available in .177 or .22 and is said to be super quiet, thanks to its fully shrouded barrel.

AIRFORCE TALONP

Airforce Airguns makes serious airguns for competition shooters and hunters. One of the newest is the TalonP, right, a PCP-powered pistol that shoots .25-caliber pellets at velocities up to 900 fps. The air tank is quick-detachable and the power is adjustable.

BROWNING 800 EXPRESS

The Browning 800 Express is available in .177-caliber at 700 fps velocity, or in .22-caliber at 600 fps. It's a spring-piston, break-barrel single-shot with a one-stroke cocking mechanism, an anti-recoil power system, and an automatic safety. A cocking assist handle is provided to give the user a bit of extra leverage. With a red dot Walther scope, we saw a shooter on YouTube get several groups with RWS Super Mag pellets under an inch at 10 meters and one at 3/8-inch, plenty enough accuracy for pest control at reasonable ranges.

UMAREX MORPH 3X

Umarex is a global company probably best known for Dynamit Nobel's RWS airguns and ammunition. It also markets airguns under its own name, like this Morph 3X, below. The name of this model relates to the design, which comes with multiple parts and converts from a pistol to a rifle. It shoots BBs and is capable of 600 fps velocity. Headquartered in Germany, with a U.S. office in Arkansas, Umarex is also licensed to manufacture airguns for some of the firearms industry's most legendary companies. These include Beretta, Browning, Colt's, Hammerli, Heckler & Koch, Magnum Research, Ruger, Smith & Wesson, a Walther. Several of these Umarex-made air rifles and pistols are included in this report.

HAMMERLI AR20 FT

Hammerli is another one of those legends in the world of firearms and airguns that has been around almost 150 years. In fact, 2013 will be the one hundred-fiftieth anniversary of this company, which was founded by Johann Hammerli, in 1863, to make rifle barrels for the Swiss Army. Hammerli rifles and pistols have won gold medals in numerous Olympic games going back to the 1950s, and the name has long been associated with high-quality, high-performance products. In 2007, Umarex began manufacturing a series of Hammerli air rifles that continues this legacy. One of these is the AR20 FT, above, a PCP competition pellet rifle. It features a Lothar Walther match-grade barrel, fully adjustable match trigger, and ambidextrous receiver and cocking piece. The stock is also fully adjustable for length, cheekpiece height, and fore-end height.

RUGER MARK I

Patterned after one of the most popular .22 rimfire pistols in history, the Mark I from Ruger, above, is a spring-piston, break-barrel air pistol in .177-caliber. This handsome, high-powered pellet pistol is made by Umarex and provides up to 500 fps velocity with a lead pellet, 600 with alloy. Its 6½-inch barrel is rifled and topped with fiber optic rear and front sights. This would make an ideal companion piece with the Standard Model .22 Long Rifle pistol that is celebrating its sixtieth anniversary in 2012.

BENJAMIN ROGUE 357 LIMITED EDITION

One of the most interesting new additions to the Benjamin catalog is the Rogue 357 Limited Edition, a .357-caliber compressed-air rifle designed specifically for hunting. It operates with ePCP technology, Benjamin's new and exclusive patent-pending system that provides a more precise and efficient regulation of the pressure. This results in more shots between refills of the reservoir. Magazine capacity is six rounds. The velocity is said to be between 700 and 1,000 fps with Nosler 127- or 145-grain bullets. The 145-grain version, incidentally, is the first airgun bullet to use Nosler's famous Ballistic Tip technology. Benjamin says the Rogue is one of the quietest air rifles on the market, thanks to its shrouded barrel. It comes with a Power Class 3-12X scope, mounting rings, and a bipod with adjustable folding legs. Early reviews brag about its superb accuracy. It's a full-size rifle at 48 inches long and weighing a bit more than nine pounds.

DAISY
POWERLINE 5170

Daisy is one of the oldest names in airguns and recently celebrated its one hundred twenty-fifth anniversary. Thankfully, the company still offers youngsters (of all ages) the Red Ryder lever-action BB gun, as well as several other air rifles specifically designed for the youth market. Daisy also makes pellet and BB rifles under the Winchester name (see separate listing), and the Daisy Powerline series of rifles and pistols. Among these is the Model 5170, above, a CO_2-powered semi-auto handgun. It comes with a 15-shot drop-out magazine and is offered in .177 or BB versions. Upper and lower rails are provided for accessories.

CROSMAN C-TT

As part of the overall growth in the popularity of airguns in general, the trend continues in look-alikes of famous powder-burning firearms. At first glance, you'd swear the C-TT is something from behind the Iron Curtain, a Tokarev TT-30. This was the main Russian Red Army service pistol from the 1930s to the '50s. Crosman's take on the Tokarev is a CO_2-powered semi-auto BB shooter with a removable 18-shot magazine, metal frame, and polymer grip. These should be showing up in your local gun store by the time you read this.

SMITH & WESSON TRR8

The Smith & Wesson TRR8 is a unique, CO_2-powered six-shot BB revolver. The steel BBs are in six removable casings that are manually loaded into a swing-out cylinder. The gun can be loaded with a speed loader that operates just like the ones use with a centerfire revolver. The fiber optic sights are adjustable, and there is an integral accessory rail under the barrel. Made by Umarex, the TRR8 is powered by a single CO_2 capsule housed in the grip. The 5½-inch barrel and two-pound weight give this model the feel of the .357 Magnum for which it is named.

WINCHESTER MODEL 11

There are many of us who are still enjoying the centennial celebration of the greatest pistol ever made. What better air pistol for fans of the John Browning classic than this one? The legendary Winchester logo makes it even more special. This is a semi-auto BB pistol made by the Daisy company under license from Winchester. It has a 16-round removable magazine and is powered by a 12-gram CO_2 cartridge. The Model 11 can be fired single- or double-action, and the slide stays open after the last shot. Overall dimensions are the same as a full-size 1911A1 centerfire pistol and the operating controls are where they should be. This is a must-have item for 1911 fans.

GAMO SILENT STALKER WHISPER

This strikingly cool rifle, dubbed by Gamo as the Silent Stalker Whisper, fires alloy pellets at velocities up to 1,200 fps and yet is very quiet. It comes with Gamo's Whisper noise dampener on the fluted and rifled polymer/steel barrel. The soft-coated synthetic stock has a palm swell and an adjustable ambidextrous cheekpiece. In addition to the fiber optic sights, the .177 rifle comes with a 3-9X scope and mount.

CROSMAN M4-177

AR-platform guns continue to be very popular in the firearms field, and that is also true with air rifles. The M4-177 from Crosman is a multi-pump pneumatic that shoots both pellets and BBs. It's tricked out with all the accessories you need for plinking, small-game hunting, and teaching the basics of shooting to beginners in the sport. Features include an adjustable stock, a variable pump action that works for right- or left-handed shooters, and a windage adjustable, dual aperture, flip-up rear sight. The front sight is elevation adjustable, and the sights can be easily removed to allow for a scope or other optics. The M4-177 uses the Firepow'r five-shot .177 pellet clips that are also used in other Crosman rifles like the Pumpmaster 760. The BB reservoir holds 350 BBs and feeds 18 of them into an internal track that goes into the action. What's that? You say you don't want a standalone airgun? Well, then, give the Crosman MAR177 PCP Conversion Kit a try. This innovative product replaces the upper on an AR/M4 firearm and converts it into a PCP air rifle. It has a removable 10-shot rotary magazine and a free-floating, rifled Lothar Walther barrel. The MAR177 is designed for National Match Air Rifle competition, and a Crosman spokesman says it is capable of match-grade accuracy. What a great idea! Now you can practice with your AR in the backyard or the basement.

CROSMAN TR77

The TR77 from Crosman is a break-barrel single-shot powered by a gas piston and has popular features like a two-stage adjustable trigger, automatic safety, and thumb-hole stock. It comes with a fixed fiber optic front sight and a fully adjustable rear, but a CenterPoint Optics 4X32mm scope is also included, ready to mount into the integral 11mm dovetail. With alloy pellets, the .177-caliber rifle is capable of 1,200 fps velocity, and 1,000 fps with lead.

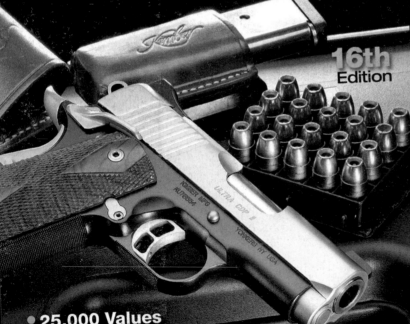